PARLIAMENTARY STUDY: LESSONS FOR GROUPS

Lessons Using *RONR (12ᵗʰ ed.)*

American Institute of Parliamentarians®

Education Department

2022

© 2020, 2022
By American Institute of Parliamentarians
(888) 664-0428
www.aipparl.org
aip@aipparl.org

Second edition
ISBN 978-1-958850-00-8
Printed June 2022
1 2 3 4 5 6 7 8 9 10

Published by the
Education Department
American Institute of Parliamentarians
W. Craig Henry, CPP-T, Education Director
Al Gage, CPP-T, President

Acknowledgements

The AIP Education Department acknowledges the parliamentarians who contributed to previous editions of a work on parliamentary study and to this book. Similar lessons for chapters were originally compiled by an AIP Education Committee chaired by Miriam Butcher, CPP. Dr. Margaret Banks, CPP; Dr. Thomas Farrar, CPP; Sally Levitan, CPP; Dr. Darwin Patnode, CPP; and Alice Pohl, CPP, also served on that committee. In 1991, the lessons were revised by Miriam Butcher, CPP, and Eve Wilkinson, a member of the board of directors. In 2002, that book was updated again by James Lochrie, CPP-T, and edited by Ann Rempel, CPP-T, AIP Education Director, and Mary Randolph, CPP-T, Education Materials Division Chair.

In 2015, using the 11th edition of RONR, Linda Juteau, CPP-T; Ann Rempel, CPP-T; Mary Remson, CPP-T; Ruth Ryan, CP-T; and Teresa Stone, CP, collaborated with Kay Allison Crews, CP, whose expertise solves all formatting problems for the department and turned the electronic files into books on parliamentary procedure under the guidance of Jeanette Williams, CP-T, AIP Education Director.

This 2022 book of parliamentary lessons for groups is based on previous contributions and updated to the 12th edition of RONR by Mary Remson, CPP-T and Joe Theobald, Ph.D, CP-T.

This page intentionally left blank

Contents

Acknowledgements v

Contents.. vii

Program Suggestions for Group Lessons..ix

Lesson 1: The Main Motion..1

Lessons 2 and 3: Amendments 11

Lesson 4: Classification and Vote Requirement of Motions 33

Lesson 5: Motion to Limit or Extend Debate and Previous Question (Close Debate and Vote Immediately) 43

Lesson 6: Practice in Reference Skills 61

Lesson 7: Decorum...71

Lessons 8 and 9: Bylaws 87

Lesson 10: Exceptions to the Rules 93

References* are indicated as:

Robert's Rules of Order Newly Revised, 12th Edition - *RONR (12th ed.)*

American Institute of Parliamentarians Standard Code of Parliamentary Procedure - AIPSC

Demeter's Manual of Parliamentary Law and Procedure - DM

* Available by ordering through www.amazon.com

This page intentionally left blank

Program Suggestions for Group Lessons

There are many ways in which the study and practice of parliamentary techniques can be approached. Varying the style can keep meetings livelier and more effective as skills are advanced and information is acquired. The following are some suggestions that any study group can use.

Students take turns in presiding at the session. After each presider's turn, constructive criticisms are made.

Students bring questions prepared in advance on a predetermined subject, give out the questions, and correct the replies. As in the game of "Charades," one team asks the questions and the other team provides the answers. Reference to textbooks (parliamentary authorities) are allowed for final proof.

Students are assigned a parliamentary subject to research such as "Nominations and Elections" or "Subsidiary Amendments" and come prepared to present and discuss their subject. During the presentation, other students ask questions designed to test the comprehensiveness of the research.

Students discuss personal experiences with meeting and parliamentary situations and ask for comments.

The workshop leader distributes prepared parliamentary questions. Students read the question aloud and answer it extemporaneously. Discussion may follow.

Students are assigned research areas using different parliamentary authorities. Findings are then compared.

Students are assigned to read a specified part of RONR (12th ed.) or AIPSC, such as the text on convention standing rules and are then required to state the information in their own words.

A special speaker may be arranged for, on occasion, from AIP or other authoritative sources.

Questions are prepared for review as true/false papers, multiple-choice selections, or to supply the missing words. It may take a format such as "Jeopardy" or similar television quiz shows.

The workshop leader distributes prepared parliamentary questions. Students must find the correct answer from among many prepared answers that have been spread out on a table. The student who matches the most questions correctly within a certain time is the winner.

Students may participate in more structured lessons as presented in the following ten lessons.

This page intentionally left blank

Lesson 1: The Main Motion

Lesson Objective:

At the end of the lesson, the student should:

1. Understand the purpose of the main motion and its characteristics.

2. Be able to define original main motions and incidental main motions and explain the differences.

3. Understand and be able to construct a resolution or main motion.

4. Be able to define several exceptions to the characteristics of main motions.

Lesson Setup:

1. The student should bring a copy of *RONR (12th ed.)*

2. The workshop leader either reads or provides a written version of the Main Motion learning activity questions.

3. The workshop leader decides whether the learning activity questions are answered one question at a time or as a total assignment. As an option, the workshop leader may assign groups of questions to smaller groups of students. In either case, the students report back in a plenary session and discuss the answers.

4. The students are then provided with the Main Motion Exceptions questions and the same process is followed, ending with a plenary session of the whole group.

5. Only the workshop leader has the answer sheet and will provide copies to all students at the end of the lesson.

Lesson Reference Material:

1. *RONR (12th ed.)*

2. Main Motion Questions (provided)

3. Main Motion– Exceptions Questions (provided)

4. Answers to 2 and 3 learning activities (provided)

Main Motion Questions:

1. The business of a meeting is carried on by means of motions. How would you define a main motion?

2. How many kinds of main motions are there? Name and define them.

3. A resolution is a main motion. What is the difference between a resolution and an ordinary main motion?

4. A main motion introduces a subject to an assembly. What subjects cannot be introduced?

5. Give examples of motions that should be ruled out of order on the grounds that they are: contrary to the bylaws, dilatory, or unsuitable for consideration.

6. What procedure can be taken to improve a main motion before action is taken?

7. How might an organization give instructions to its employees?

8. There are some incidental main motions that have been given specific names and may have some individual characteristics and rules differing from those of other main motions. List some common incidental main motions with specific names.

9. Subsidiary motions assist the assembly in treating or disposing of a main motion. List the incidental main motions corresponding to subsidiary motions.

10. Privileged motions do not relate to the pending business but have to do with matters of immediate or overriding importance. List the incidental main motions corresponding to privileged motions.

Answers to Main Motion (*RONR (12th ed.)*) Questions:

1. The business of a meeting is carried on by means of motions. How would you define a main motion?

   RONR (12th ed.) 6:1, 10:1. A main motion is a motion whose introduction brings business before the assembly.

2. How many kinds of main motions are there? Name and define them.

   RONR (12th ed.) 10:4. There are two kinds of main motions: the *original main motion* and the *incidental main motion*. The original main motion is a motion that introduces a substantive question as a new subject. The incidental main motion is a main motion that is incidental to or relates to the business of the assembly or its past or future action. It does not mark the beginning of a particular involvement of the assembly in a substantive matter, as an original main motion does.

3. A resolution is a main motion. What is the difference between a resolution and an ordinary main motion?

   RONR (12th ed.) 10:13. A resolution is an original main motion submitted in writing beginning with the word "Resolved." A resolution can consist of more than one resolving clause. Another difference is that, although it is inadvisable to attempt to include reasons for a motion's adoption within the statement of the motion, in a resolution the background or reasons for the motion's adoption may be written as a preamble and placed before the resolving clause.

   (See ***AIPSC*, pp. 36-37,** for information about the resolution form.)

4. A main motion introduces a subject to an assembly. What subjects cannot be introduced?

   RONR (12th ed.) 10:26.

   a. No main motion is in order that conflicts with the corporate charter, constitution, or bylaws (although a main motion to amend them may be in order; see RONR (12th ed.) 35, 57); and to the extent that procedural rules applicable to the organization or assembly are prescribed by federal, state, or local law, no main motion is in order that conflicts with such rules.

   b. A motion that proposes action outside the scope of the organization's object as defined in the corporate charter, constitution, or bylaws is not in order unless the assembly by a two-thirds vote authorizes its introduction.

   c. No main motion is in order that presents substantially the same question as a motion that was finally disposed of earlier in the same session by being rejected, postponed indefinitely (11), or subjected to an *Objection to the Consideration of a Question* (26) that was sustained.

d. Apart from a motion to *Rescind* or to *Amend Something Previously Adopted* (35), no main motion is in order that conflicts with a motion previously adopted at any time and still in force. If a main motion that interferes with a desired action has been adopted, a motion to *Reconsider* (37) the vote on it can be made for a limited time during the same session; and if it is reconsidered, it can be voted down or amended as desired, in the reconsideration.

e. No main motion is in order that would conflict with or that presents substantially the same question as one which has been *temporarily but not finally disposed of*—whether in the same or an earlier session—and which remains *within the control of the assembly.* (see RONR (12th ed.) 9:7-11, 38:8). Also in any assembly, a main motion that has been referred to a committee cannot be renewed until after the session at which the assembly finally disposes of the main motion – after the committee has reported it back or has been discharged from its consideration.

5. Give examples of motions that should be ruled out of order on the grounds that they are: contrary to the bylaws, dilatory, or unsuitable for consideration.

    Answers will vary. See ***RONR (12th ed.) 10:26-27, 13:9, 39:1-7***

6. What procedure can be taken to improve a main motion before action is taken?

    RONR (12th ed.) 4:20, 10:30(1). After a main motion has been made but before the chair states it or rules it is not in order, no debate is in order. However, any member can quickly rise and without waiting to be recognized informally suggest one or more modifications in the motion, which, at this point the maker can accept or reject as he wishes. (4:20-22)

    RONR (12th ed.) 10:30(2). After the question has been stated by the chair – although the assembly, and not the maker of the motion, then has control over its wording – the maker can request unanimous consent to modify the motion. (33:11-19).

    RONR (12th ed.) 10:30(3). By means of the subsidiary motion to *Amend*, (12), members can propose changes to be made in the wording and, within limits, the meaning of a pending main motion before it is voted on.

RONR (12ᵗʰ ed.) 10:30(3)(b). The motion to *Substitute* an entire new text of the main motion in place of the pending version. (Also **RONR (12ᵗʰ ed.) 12:69-90**

RONR (12ᵗʰ ed.) 10:30(4). The subsidiary motion to *Commit (Refer)* can be used to refer the main motion to committee if the main motion requires time or study. (See **RONR (12ᵗʰ ed.) 13**)

RONR (12ᵗʰ ed.) 10:30(5). A member speaking in debate can urge rejection of the pending main motion, saying that if it is voted down he will offer a different main motion, which he can describe briefly and which deals with the general problem in a substantially different way.

7.   How might an organization give instructions to its employees?

RONR (12ᵗʰ ed.) 10:24. The organization may instruct employees through an *order* which is written just as a resolution, except that the word *Ordered* is used in place of the word *Resolved*.

8.   There are some incidental main motions that have been given specific names and may have some individual characteristics and rules differing from those of other main motions. List some common incidental main motions with specific names.

RONR (12ᵗʰ ed.) 6:27(2). The motion to *Rescind* or to *Amend Something Previously Adopted* is an incidental main motion because it brings business before the assembly by its introduction. See **RONR (12ᵗʰ ed.) (35)**, **RONR (12ᵗʰ ed.) t14, (34, 35)**. The motion to *Discharge a Committee* is an incidental main motion. (See **RONR (12ᵗʰ ed.) 36:1-15.**)

RONR (12ᵗʰ ed.) 10:5, 10:52-57. The motion to *Ratify* is an incidental main motion.

9.   Subsidiary motions assist the assembly in treating or disposing of a main motion. List the incidental main motions corresponding to subsidiary motions.

RONR (12ᵗʰ ed.) 6:9. For each of the subsidiary motions *Amend, Commit, Postpone Definitely,* and *Limit or Extend Limits of Debate*, there is a corresponding incidental main motion (10:4-5) of the same name that can be made when no other motion is pending.

RONR (12ᵗʰ ed.) t8 (#13), 6:27(2), (35). The motion to *Amend Something Previously Adopted* is an incidental main motion and requires a two-thirds vote or a majority vote of the entire membership unless previous notice is given.

***RONR (12th ed.)* t12 (#27), t22 (#69), 13:6, 14:3.** The motions to *Commit* and *Postpone to a Certain Time* when no business is pending are incidental main motions.

***RONR (12th ed.)* t14 (#33), 10:7, 15:4.** The motion to *Limit or Extend Limits of Debate* made when no business is pending is an incidental main motion.

10. Privileged motions do not relate to the pending business but have to do with matters of immediate or overriding importance. List the incidental main motions corresponding to privileged motions.

***RONR (12th ed.)* t24 (#73), 6:13, (19).** A **Question of Privilege,** if raised when no motion is pending is an incidental main motion. (Note: Do not confuse a question of privilege with the device "Raise a Question of Privilege," which is the privileged motion.) 6:12(2), 19:1n2

***RONR (12th ed.)* t26 (#80), 10:7, (20).** The motion to **Recess** made when no business is pending is an incidental main motion.

***RONR (12th ed.)* t6 (#3), 6:13, (21).** A motion to **Adjourn** may be a privileged or a main motion depending on a number of conditions. Adjourn when qualified in any way, or having the effect of dissolving the assembly is treated as any other main motion.

***RONR (12th ed.)* t16 (#43), 6:13, (22).** A motion to **Fix the Time to Which to Adjourn** may be a main motion if proposed when no question is pending.

Summary:

The real difference between an original main motion and an incidental main motion is that the original main motion brings *new* business before the assembly for consideration and action. Another difference is that the *Objection to the Consideration* may be applied to an original main motion, but it cannot be applied to an incidental main motion.

Main Motion Exceptions:

Find the answers to the following questions in *RONR (12th ed.)*. Write the exception(s) and cite the reference with section and paragraph numbers.

1.   A main motion must be seconded before it is open for discussion, except?

2.   Main motions may be reconsidered, except?

3.   Main motions require a majority vote for adoption, except?

4.   Only one main motion can be pending at a given time, except?

5.   A resolution may be adopted by a majority vote, except?

Answers to Exceptions (*RONR (12th ed.)*):

Find the answers to the following questions in *RONR (12th ed.)*. Write the exception(s) and cite the reference with section and paragraph numbers.

1. A main motion must be seconded before it is open for discussion, except?

   RONR (12th ed.) 7:2(4). When the motion is made by direction of a board or committee.

   RONR (12th ed.) 4:9n7. Motions need not be seconded in a small board or committee.

   RONR (12th ed.) t44. Some *requests* when stated as a main motion do not require a second. For example, a motion to grant a request of another member to be excused from a duty. **32:2(4).**

2. The vote on main motions may be reconsidered, except?

   RONR (12th ed.) 37:9(2).

   a. A motion which can be renewed; (see 38:6-7).

   b. A negative vote on a motion which, at the time the motion to *Reconsider* is made, would be out of order because:

      i. it conflicts with a motion previously adopted and still in force,

      ii. it conflicts with a motion which has been temporarily but not finally disposed of and which remains within the control of the assembly, or

      iii. it would conflict with a pending motion if that motion were adopted;

   c. An affirmative vote whose provisions have been partly carried out;

   d. An affirmative vote in the nature of a contract when the party to the contract has been notified of the outcome;

   e. Any vote which has caused something to be done that it is impossible to undo;

   f. A vote on a motion to *Reconsider*

   g. An election that has become final as provided in 46:46; or

   h. When practically the same result as desired can be obtained by some other parliamentary motion that can be adopted by majority vote without previous notice.

3. Main motions require a majority vote for adoption, except?

RONR (12ᵗʰ ed.) 10:8(7).

a.   When the motion proposes an action for which the bylaws or special rules of order prescribe a requirement of more than a majority vote.

b.   When adoption of the motion would have the effect of suspending a rule of order or a parliamentary right of members, in which cases it requires a two-thirds vote.

c.   When adoption of the motion would have the effect of changing something already adopted.

4.   Only one main motion can be pending at a given time, except?

RONR (12ᵗʰ ed.) 6:17(5). When the main motion is divided. (See also **Division of a Question (27)**.

RONR (12ᵗʰ ed.) 19:3. When a question of privilege has been admitted by the chair and is in the form of a main motion it may be dealt with immediately, notwithstanding that it interrupted the pending business (which may be another main motion).

5.   A resolution may be adopted by a majority vote, except?

RONR (12ᵗʰ ed.) 8:14. When there is a resolution to amend bylaws or rules of order that require a two-thirds vote.

RONR (12ᵗʰ ed.) 10:8(7).

a.   when the motion proposes an action for which the bylaws or special rules of order prescribe a requirement of more than a majority vote;

b.   when adoption of the motion would have the effect of suspending a rule of order or a parliamentary right of members, in which case it requires a two-thirds vote;

c.   when adoption of the motion would have the effect of changing something already adopted.

Lessons 2 and 3: Amendments

Lesson Objective:

At the end of the two lessons the student should:

1. Understand the purpose of amendments and their characteristics.

2. Understand the three basic methods of making amendments, including the substitute amendment.

3. Understand the process of handling amendments including primary and secondary amendments.

4. Understand the concept of germaneness of amendments.

5. Be able to handle main motions and amendments while acting as a presiding officer.

Lesson Setup:

1. The student should bring a copy of *RONR (12th ed.)*

2. The students may do learning activity 3 and 4 individually, it is recommended that the students discuss the answers as a group. The students can also be broken into two or more discussion groups.

3. The Article on Amendments is discussed and clarified at the meeting prior to the Questions on Amendments being handed out. The group answers the questions and refers to *RONR (12th ed.)* to verify the answers.

4. The learning activity on Germaneness of Amendments is handed out and answered as a group.

5. The learning activity on Practice Presiding on Amendments is handed out and the students' practice.

6. The workshop leader has the answers for learning activities 3, 4, and 5 below, which are not handed out until the lessons are complete.

Lesson Reference Material:

1. *RONR (12th ed.)*

2. Article on Amendments (provided)

3. Germaneness Quiz (provided)

4. Questions on Amendments (provided)

5. Practice Presiding on Amendments (provided)

6. Answers to 3, 4, and 5 (provided)

Article on Amendments:

Quite often it becomes necessary to change the wording of a main motion before members are willing to make a final decision on it. As discussion develops, it can become evident that the original main motion is inadequate, incomplete, or ineptly stated. The motion needs to be changed somewhat, modified in some way to make it acceptable. Members may like the basic idea as expressed in the motion but become convinced that there is need for improvement or change. This is done by amending. The intent of amending, then, is to improve upon, perfect, or complete the action desired in the main motion to all the members' satisfaction. The motion to amend belongs to the main motion.

RONR (12th ed.) 's definition of the subsidiary motion to *Amend* is: "...a motion to modify the wording–and within certain limits the meaning – of a pending motion before the pending motion itself is acted upon." **RONR (12th ed.), p. 12:1.**

Amend is a subsidiary motion, sixth in rank. **RONR (12th ed.), pp. 12:3-4, t4.** As much attention should be paid to it as to the main motion itself. Next to the main motion, it is the most widely used of all motions, but it is also too often misused because it has several forms and the proper use of them is not always understood. It pays to study thoroughly the ways in which a main motion may be amended, how each form is used and to be familiar with its characteristics. If you ever have participated in a brainstorming session where everyone throws in ideas regardless of merit, and have seen the process pick apart ideas, retaining the best and discarding the poorest, you will understand the purpose of amendments. Amending, however, is a parliamentary procedure and, while it accomplishes the same purpose, is more formal in style – it is not a brainstorming session.

RONR (12th ed.), 33:12-13. To save time, amendments are sometimes accepted informally *before* the motion has been stated by the chair. If the maker of the motion calls out "I agree" or "I will accept that," the chair states the question on the modified motion. *After* a motion has been stated by the chair, it belongs to the meeting as a whole, and the maker of the motion must request the assembly's permission to modify his own motion. The chair says: "Unless there is objection, the motion is modified." If there is no objection, the motion is amended by unanimous (general) consent. If there is an objection, the amendment is put to a vote.

Amendments are themselves amendable and are also debatable if the main motion is debatable. The subsidiary motion to *Amend* can be reconsidered and yields to all subsidiary motions except the motion to *Postpone Indefinitely*, which has a lower rank. The subsidiary motion to *Amend* is adopted by a majority vote even if the main motion requires a two-thirds vote for adoption. Opponents of the main motion that is being amended will have the opportunity to defeat the main motion as amended in the final vote. For example, a motion to amend the bylaws (a main motion) requires a two-thirds vote but the amendment to that main motion requires only a majority vote.

No amendment may stand by itself. It owes its existence to the main motion.

Any member can participate in proposing changes and alterations. Any member may even amend his or her own motion. Any member can ask the chair for assistance in properly wording an amendment in the desired form. A member's vote on an amendment does not obligate the member to vote the same way on the main motion, whether amended or not.

There are three basic processes or forms (*RONR (12th ed.)*, 13:8) to amend plus the method of filling blanks (***RONR (12th ed.)*, 12:92-113**), which is not really a motion to amend but is often used for its relation to amending.

Form 1:   To insert or add a word or consecutive words or a paragraph.
            ***RONR (12th ed.)*, 12:8(1), 12:26, 12:31.**
            Example: Main Motion (M.M.). "I move that we buy a TV for our recreation room."
            Amend, to insert: "I move that we insert the word 'smart' before the word 'TV.'"

Form 2:   To strike out a word, or consecutive words or a paragraph.
            ***RONR (12th ed.)*, 12:8(2), 12:46, 12:51.**
            Example of strike out: M.M. "I move that we buy a silk flag for our entrance hall."
            Amend: "I move to strike out the word 'silk' before the word 'flag.'"

Form 3:   To strike out and insert, a combination of both. ***RONR (12th ed.)*, pp. 134, 149-162.**
            Example: M.M. "I move that we buy a used computer for our office."
            Amend: "I move that we strike out the word 'used' and insert the words 'new Dell laptop' before the word 'computer.'"

Notice the use of the words "strike out" instead of the word "delete." Delete means erase, destroy. *RONR (12th ed.)* prefers "strike out" as a more accurate term.

Words may be added at the end of a main motion in the method of inserting.

Striking out and inserting, and many **other** amendments may create such confusion that the original motion with its amendments becomes too involved. In that case, the original motion may be struck out and a new one, called a *substitute*, may be offered in its place.

To **substitute** is to strike out an entire motion or paragraph and insert another one in its place. ***RONR (12th ed.)*, 12:57, 12:69-90.**

To *substitute* requires the use of a complete paragraph (which may be as short as one sentence) and is not to be confused with striking out and inserting a few words. In the latter case, the term "substitute" is never used.

Example of a substitute amendment:

Main Motion:	"I move that flower beds be set in the N.E. Quadrangle." Amended to insert "four" before "flower beds." Amended to add "displaying annuals and perennials." Later amended to add "to be formed into a square."
Substitute Amendment:	"I move that the school gardener be directed to draw up and submit to the next Grounds Committee meeting, plans and specifications for adequate flower beds in the N.E. Quadrangle."

There are rules for these different processes. They should be very carefully studied to permit flexibility and protection from too many amendments being offered unnecessarily.

To **insert or add**: The words should be accurate and can be perfected by means of a secondary amendment that will be discussed next. The words to be desired must be the right ones since, once they are inserted, they can only be changed by reconsideration, or by amendments presenting a new question, such as a substitute.

To **strike out words**: The exact location must be clear, and this motion can only be applied to a word or consecutive words. Separated words can be struck out by separate motions or by inserting a new clause that include the separated words to be struck.

To **strike out and insert**: The two parts of this motion cannot be separated in the manner of a division or a question but must be treated as one motion. Although it is not in order to strike out in one place and insert in another to obtain something materially different by the use of this motion, it sometimes may be done if unanimous (general) consent is granted to do so.

To **substitute**: This form of amendment is a useful, effective, valuable means to clarify the action desired, especially where there has been confusion. In such a case, a member may speak against the pending amendment and say that if it is rejected the member is prepared to offer a substitute motion. Once the substitution has been proposed, it becomes the primary amendment and debate can go on into the merits of the main motion as well as the substitute. The chair reads both the present substitute and the original motion. Then the proponents of the original motion are given first opportunity to amend their proposition to a more acceptable form as revealed necessary by the introduction of a substitute. The substitute itself may have an amendment applied to it. After debate and amendments both motions are read, usually by the chair and the chair then puts the vote on the motion last read, the substitute "Shall the motion last read be substituted for the pending main motion?" If it is accepted in preference to the pending main motion, the question is now on adopting the substitute as the will of the assembly.

If the motion to amend by substitution is lost, the vote is on the pending motion (as amended). "The motion to *substitute* often provides a convenient and timesaving method for handling a poorly framed resolution, or for introducing a different and better approach to the real question raised by the main motion." ***RONR (12th ed.), 12:79.***

There are two degrees of amendments. An amendment to a main motion is considered a primary amendment. One amendment can be applied to the primary amendment and is a secondary amendment – not to be confused with secondary motions.

The *primary amendment* applies directly to the main motion and must be germane to it. The *secondary amendment* applies to the primary amendment and must be germane to it. To avoid confusion, after that, no more amendments may be applied at that time, i.e., no tertiary amendments.

We can, therefore, amend amendments, but this is where certain restrictions must start. Limitations must be placed on the consequence of one amendment after another that make for confusion and would snarl and delay the meeting.

The two amendments, primary and secondary, are considered in reverse order to their proposal. First, the secondary amendment is decided upon, then the primary amendment, and then the main motion as amended. Remember: one thing at a time – we resolve one amendment at a time.

Example of a secondary amendment:

Main Motion:	"I move that we buy a silk flag."
Primary amendment.	"I move that we strike out the word 'silk' and insert 'nylon' before the word 'flag.'"
Secondary amendment:	"I move that we insert the words 'parachute-quality' before the word 'nylon.'"

There is *no limit* to the number of amendments that may be applied to a main motion so long as only one amendment is pending at a time except in the case of a primary and secondary amendment, in which case the secondary amendment is the immediately pending motion.

Another reminder: When an amendment has been adopted, it does *not* mean that the main motion has been adopted. The main question must then be voted on as amended.

All **amendments must be germane,** relevant, and appropriate. *Germane* means that the amendment must in some way be involved with the question and owe its existence to the question. It cannot introduce an independent question. The amendment can even be hostile to the main motion although it cannot negate it. Negation is achieved by defeating the motion. *RONR (12th ed.),* **12:16-21.**

Example

Main Motion:	"I move to commend the president for his prompt response to criticism by the news media."
Amend:	"I move to strike out the word 'commend' and insert the word 'condemn'."
(In order)	

Or

Main Motion:	"I move that we ratify action taken by our financial secretary."
Amend:	"I move that we strike out 'ratify' and insert 'deny support of' before the word 'action'."
(Not in order)	

The first example is in order because it is hostile; the second is out of order because it is the same as negating the motion and can be accomplished by voting down the pending main motion.

Usually there is no problem with germaneness. Common sense tells us whether or not we are talking about the same thing, but sometimes it becomes difficult to determine. If it becomes necessary, the chair makes the ruling on germaneness and the ruling may be appealed. If the chair is in doubt, the decision may be submitted to the assembly, from which there is no appeal. A rule of thumb for germaneness is that the part (being added or inserted) must relate to the whole.

There are two procedures, to be mentioned only in brief in this lesson, that are so closely related to the motion to amend that they cannot be overlooked.

1. **Filling Blanks: *RONR (12th ed.),* 12:92-113.** As has been said, filling blanks is not a form of amendment but it is, to quote *RONR (12th ed.),* "a device by which an unlimited number of alternative choices for a particular specification **in a main motion or primary amendment** can be pending at the same time" (emphasis added), which eliminates the sometime disadvantage of allowing only primary and secondary amendments. In other words, it provides an exception to the rule permitting only two amendments at one time. When regular

amendments are proposed, three alternatives may be considered; the secondary amendment, the primary amendment and the main motion. But with filling blanks, any number may be submitted for the final selection. Cases adaptable for such treatment are a selection of names, places, dates, numbers, or amounts.

A member moves to create a blank which requires a second, is not amendable or debatable, and requires a majority vote. If the creation of the blank is adopted, the members may then offer different names or numbers according to the category under consideration. These are then voted upon in a chosen, logical order and, according to **RONR (12ᵗʰ ed.), 12:96**, the first one receiving a majority vote fills the blank. The main motion must then be voted on as amended.

(Note that **AIPSC, pp. 55-56,** fills blanks by voting on all choices, and the choice that received the highest majority fills the blank. The main motion must then be voted on as amended.)

Amend Something Previously Adopted: RONR (12ᵗʰ ed.), 35:1-13. This incidental main motion has a specific use, the effect of which is to modify previous adopted action and, on occasion, to replace that action by substituting some other action. **Rescind** is subject to the same rules as the motion to *Amend Something Previously Adopted.*

There are amendments that must be considered out of order or *improper* – such as an amendment that is not germane; one that negates the main motion; any amendments that would be identical with one previously adopted; or one that proposes to change the form of amendment, convert it to another parliamentary motion, or that is dilatory. Amendments that conflict with procedural rules contained in statutory laws are also, of course, to be ruled out of order. **RONR (12ᵗʰ ed.), 12:22, 39:1-7.**

(Note that **AIPSC, pp. 50-58,** treats amendments differently and in particular substitute amendments and filling blanks while **DM, pp. 68-82,** treats amendments similar to *RONR (12ᵗʰ ed.)*.)

Questions on Amendments:

1. Define an amendment.

2. State the forms of amendment.

3. What are the degrees of an amendment?

4. What does *germane* mean?

5. What is a secondary amendment?

6. Which of the amendments is voted on first?

7. If the amendment is adopted what happened to the main motion?

8. How is germaneness determined?

9. How is a substitute amendment handled?

10. Are all amendments acceptable? Why or why not?

11. What are the Standard Descriptive Characteristics of *Amend*?

12. When is an amendment to a preamble in order?

13. Who amends motions?

14. What is the advantage of using the motion to *Create a Blank*?

15. Can a member move to "delete" part of a motion?

16. If a motion to *Strike Out and Insert* is voted down, what is in order?

17. What motion contradicts Standard Descriptive Characteristic #6 of the subsidiary motion to *Amend*?

18. What is the purpose of the motion to *Amend*?

19. If a member votes no on an amendment, must the member vote no on the main motion?

20. What is meant by a hostile amendment?

21. Why is a substitute motion often well used?

22. When a blank is to be filled with a name, in what order does the chair present the names?

23. How is an amendment to the bylaws treated?

24. Once a substitute motion has been offered, what is the next action taken by the chair?

25. How is a substitute motion treated so as to be fair to both sides?

Germaneness of Amendments – Quiz:

Are the following amendments, proposed individually, germane? YES OR NO? (Mark yes or no for each subsection of the main motion.)

1. Main motion pending "to increase the secretary's salary $50 more per month."

    a. and also buy him a desk not to exceed $75 _____

    b. to be retroactive to last January _____

    c. and also buy a new gavel for the president _____

    d. and congratulate him on his excellent work as secretary _____

2. Main motion pending "to paint the club library green."

    a. the cost not to exceed $500 _____

    b. and buy a new encyclopedia for our library _____

    c. the work to be done by union labor _____

    d. and the executive board shall henceforth meet in the library _____

    e. and air-condition our meeting room _____

3. Main motion pending "to build our headquarters at the corner of A and B Streets."

    a. and buy the lot across the street for a parking area _____

    b. and have two passenger elevators and one freight elevator _____

    c. and air-condition the entire building _____

    d. and hang a picture of our national president in the meeting room _____

    e. and for income, lease the basement floor to McDonald's _____

4. Main motion pending "to invite the senior U.S. Senator to address our annual convention."

    a. provided the Governor can come on our opening day _____

    b. and commend him on his work for our state in Congress _____

    c. and request him not to play golf on a public golf course _____

    d. and suggest that the Governor resign to take a Supreme Court judgeship _____

    e. and that the two vice-presidents escort him to the platform _____

5. Main motion pending "to hold our annual April dinner dance at the Waldorf."

    a. to be preceded by a cocktail hour _____

    b. and ask the Governor to be our speaker _____

    c. and instruct the board to offer $10 million to buy the Waldorf _____ _____

    d. and request the management to provide waiters and waitresses __ _____

    e. and have an opportunity to visit the kitchens one half hour before dinner _____

Practice Presiding on Amendments (RONR (12ᵗʰ ed.)):

Instructions: Assign a student or request a volunteer to preside for each question, use a different student for each scenario presented below. The other students should act as the members in the meeting. They should make the motions and vote when required. Stick to the scenario and the order as it is given. (Guidelines for these activities are provided in the Answer Section.)

1. John Adams of the Northtown Improvement Association offered the motion to improve the city park by cutting the grass and weeds, filling washed out cavities with sand, and replacing the fence.

    Pat Baker moved to amend the motion by striking out the word "replacing" and inserting the word "repairing."

    Harry Black offered an amendment to add "with the same kind of fencing" after the word "repairing."

    Tom Jones moved to substitute "filling washed out cavities" with "placing drain tile in the cavities and cover the sidewalks."

2. Robert Macho moved that the annual meeting be a supper meeting.

    Tom Chauvin moved to amend the motion by adding "and that the supper be prepared by the hospitality committee" after the word "meeting."

    Dick Byers moved to amend the amendment by adding "and that they be reimbursed for the costs from our treasury."

    John Jones moved that this be amended by striking out "for the costs from our treasury" and inserting "by charging a fee of $48.00 from each member attending the meeting."

    Vera Smart moved to substitute: "That the annual meeting be a buffet supper meeting that shall be catered by our local Bon Appetit Caterers.

    Ima Practical moved to amend the substitute by adding "the cost not to exceed $48.00 per member."

Answers to Questions on Amendments:

Answers are given on this sheet but should not be read to the students who are studying the lesson. The object is to have the students find the identifying pages themselves.

1. Define an amendment.

    RONR (12th ed.), 12:1. The subsidiary motion to *Amend* is a motion to modify the wording—and within certain limits the meaning—of a pending motion before the pending motion itself is acted upon.

2. State the forms of amendment.

    RONR (12th ed.), 12:8. There are three basic processes of amendment, the third of which is an indivisible combination of the first two. The three forms are: (1) to *insert*, or to *add*; (2) to *strike out* (words or a paragraph); and (3) to strike out and insert (substitute, that is to strike out a paragraph, or entire text, and insert another in its place).

3. What are the degrees of an amendment?

    RONR (12th ed.), 12:11-13. The subsidiary motion to amend can, in general, be amended, so that two degrees of amendment—primary and secondary—are possible. A primary amendment applies directly to a pending motion; a secondary amendment applies to a pending primary amendment.

4. What does *germane* mean?

    RONR (12th ed.), 12:6, 12:16-21. An amendment must always be *germane*—that is, closely related to or having bearing on the subject of the motion to be amended. To be *germane*, an amendment must *in some way involve* the same question that is raised by the motion to which it is applied. When a secondary amendment proposes a change in the primary amendment, it must be germane *to that primary amendment*—not just to the motion the primary amendment would change. An amendment cannot introduce an independent question; but can be hostile to the spirit of the original motion and still be germane.

5. What is a secondary amendment?

    RONR (12th ed.), 1:7(2), 12:11-13. A secondary amendment is an amendment to an amendment. A secondary amendment applies to a pending primary amendment; it proposes a change in the primary amendment or, in certain cases, in a paragraph that the primary amendment proposes to strike out of the pending motion. A secondary amendment is sometimes called an *amendment of the second degree*.

6. Which of the amendments is voted on first?

    RONR (12th ed.), 5:7-8. That the secondary amendment is voted on first may be inferred from the wording in this section and paragraph numbers.

7. If the amendment is adopted what happened to the main motion?
   RONR (12th ed.), 12:4. Adoption of a subsidiary motion to *Amend* does *not* adopt the motion thereby amended; that motion remains pending in its modified form.

8. How is germaneness determined?
   RONR (12th ed.), 12:16-21. These general rules of parliamentary law can be applied: (1) During the session in which the assembly has decided a question, another main motion raising the same or substantially the same question cannot be introduced. (2) While a motion has been temporarily disposed of (as explained in RONR (12th ed.), 9:9), no other motion can be admitted that might conflict with one of the possible final decisions on the first motion. If a proposed amendment is related to the main motion in such a way that, after the adoption, rejection, or temporary disposal of the present main motion, the essential idea of the amendment could not be introduced as an independent resolution during the same session, the amendment is germane and should be admitted, since there will not, or may not, be an opportunity to present it later. There are borderline cases where a presiding officer will find it difficult to judge the germaneness of an amendment. Whenever in doubt, he should admit the amendment or, in important cases, refer the decision to the assembly.

9. How is a substitute amendment handled?
   RONR (12th ed.), 12:82-91. A substitute can be offered for a paragraph or a main motion of only one sentence. A primary amendment to substitute is open to debate at all times while it is pending with no secondary amendment pending; and such debate may go fully into the merits of both the original text and the substitute. When a motion to *substitute* is under consideration, the paragraph to be struck out as well as the paragraph to be inserted can be perfected by secondary amendment in any of the three basic forms. The chair has the option of accepting only amendments to the paragraph to be struck out first, and then only amendments to the proposed substitute. After all secondary amendments have been disposed of and after any further debate on the motion to substitute, the vote is taken on whether to make this substitution.

10. Are all amendments acceptable? Why or why not?
    RONR (12th ed.), 12:22. The following types of amendments are out of order: (1) one that is not germane; (2) one that merely makes the adoption of the amended question equivalent to a rejection of the original motion; (3) one that would cause the question as amended to be out of order; (4) one that proposes to change of the forms of

amendment into another form; (5) one that would have the effect of converting one parliamentary motion into another; and (6) one that strikes out the word *"Resolved"* or other enacting words.

11. What are the Standard Descriptive Characteristics of *Amend*?

    RONR (12ᵗʰ ed.), 12:7. (1) When *applied to a main motion*, takes precedence over the main motion and over the subsidiary motion to *Postpone Indefinitely* and yields to all subsidiary motions other than *Postpone Indefinitely* and *Amend* (yields to a motion to *Amend* that is applied to it), yields to all privileged motions and applicable incidental motions; when applied to other than a main motions, it takes precedence over the motion that it proposes to amend; yields to any privileged or subsidiary motion (other than *Amend*) to which that motions that it proposes to amend would yield, also yields to motions to *Amend*, to *Limit or Extend Limits of Debate,* or to the *Previous Question* that are applied to it, and yields to all applicable incidental motions; (2) Can be applied to any main motion and to any other motion that contains a variable factor; (3) is out of order when another has the floor; (4) must be seconded; (5) is debatable whenever the motion to which it is applied is debatable; (6) is generally amendable; (7) requires a majority vote, regardless of the vote required to adopt the question to be amended; (8) can be reconsidered.

12. When is an amendment to a preamble in order?

    RONR (12ᵗʰ ed.), 12:23. The preamble of a resolution is not opened to amendment until after amendment of the resolving clauses has been completed. After any amendment of the preamble, a single vote is taken on the question of adopting the entire resolution or paper.

13. Who amends motions?

    RONR (12ᵗʰ ed.), 12:5. The assembly, by majority vote, amends motions.

14. What is the advantage of using the motion to *Create a Blank*?

    RONR (12ᵗʰ ed.), 12:92-93. Creating a blank is a device by which an unlimited number of alternative choices for a particular specification in a main motion or primary amendment can be pending at the same time. In effect, it permits an exception to the rule that only one primary and one secondary amendment can be pending at a time.

15. Can a member move to "delete" part of a motion?

    RONR (12ᵗʰ ed.), 12:8(2)(n3). The application of the word "delete" to any form of amendment is not a preferred parliamentary usage, but the shortened expression "to strike" is acceptable.

16. If a motion to *Strike Out and Insert* is voted down, what is in order?

    RONR (12ᵗʰ ed.), 12:64. If a motion to strike out and insert is voted down, it is still in order: (1) to make either of the separate motions to *strike out,* or to *insert,* the same words that would have been struck out or inserted by the combine motion that was lost; and (2) to make another motion to *strike out and insert*—provided that the change in either the wording to be struck out or the wording to be inserted presents a question materially different from the one that was voted down.

17. What motion contradicts Standard Descriptive Characteristic #6 of the subsidiary motion to *Amend*?

    RONR (12ᵗʰ ed.), 12:92. Filling Blanks is a device by which an unlimited number of alternative choices can be pending at the same time.

18. What is the purpose of the motion to *Amend*?

    RONR (12ᵗʰ ed.), 6:5(2). To make the wording (and within certain limits the meaning) of a pending motion more suitable or acceptable in an altered form before the main motion is voted on.

19. If a member votes no on an amendment, must the member vote no on the main motion?

    RONR (12ᵗʰ ed.), 12:5. A member's vote on an amendment does not obligate him to vote in a particular way on the motion to which the amendment applies; he is free to vote as he pleases on the main motion, whether it is amended or not.

20. What is meant by a hostile amendment?

    RONR (12ᵗʰ ed.), 12:16, 12:20. A hostile amendment is one that is antagonistic to the original intent of the motion it proposes to amend.

21. Why is a substitute motion often well used?

    RONR (12ᵗʰ ed.), 12:79. The motion to *substitute* often provides a convenient and timesaving method for handling a poorly framed resolution, or for introducing a different and better approach to the real question raised by a main motion. Properly applied, the rules for the treatment of motions to *substitute* automatically operate in fairness to both sides when there is disagreement about the preference of the original or the substitute.

22. When a blank is to be filled with a name, in what order does the chair present the names?

    RONR (12ᵗʰ ed.), 12:107(a). The procedure for filling a blank with one name is practically the same as for making nominations. The chair repeats each name as it is proposed, and finally takes a vote on each in the same order, until one receives a majority.

23. How is an amendment to the bylaws treated?

    RONR (12ᵗʰ ed.), 55:1. A motion to amend the bylaws is a particular case of the motion to *Amend Something Previously Adopted;* it is therefore a main motion, and it is subject to the same rules as other motions with certain exceptions: (1) the requirements for amendment specified in the bylaws must be adhered to; (2) permissible primary and secondary amendment of the motion to amend the bylaws is usually limited by the extent of change for which notice was given; (3) an affirmative vote on the motion to amend the bylaws cannot be reconsidered; (4) the rule that, when a main motion is adopted, no other conflicting main motion is thereafter in order is not applicable to the motion to amend the bylaws, since several notices of proposals representing different approaches to the same problem may have been given, and all such bylaw amendments are entitled to be considered.

24. Once a substitute motion has been offered, what is the next action taken by the chair?
   RONR (12th ed.), 12:71. The chair states the substitute and opens the original text to amendment.

25. How is a substitute motion treated so as to be fair to both sides?
   RONR (12th ed.), 12:81. The chair opens the original text to amendment and after debate and amendment, accepts amendments to the proposed substitute. Thus, both sides have opportunity to amend their proposition into a more acceptable form and for their proposition to receive appropriate consideration.

Answers to Quiz on Germaneness of Amendments:

1. b and d yes.

2. a and c yes.

3. b and c yes.

4. a, b, and e yes.

5. a, b, d, and e yes.

Answers to Practice Presiding on Amendments:

Assume all motions have been seconded.

1. John Adams moved the main motion.

   Pat Baker moved a primary amendment.

   Harry Black moved a secondary amendment, germane to the primary amendment.

   Tom Jones' motion to substitute, should be ruled out of order at this time, as the rule for amending is that no motion can have more than two amendments pending at one time. (RONR (12th ed.), 12:12) After the pending amendments have been disposed, Tom may offer his amendment as new primary amendment. It cannot be moved as a new secondary amendment as it is not germane to "replacing" the fence. NOTE: Tom's motion is to amend by striking and inserting words – it is NOT a substitute amendment because it does not apply to a paragraph. The student assigned the role of Tom Jones should be instructed to use the correct parliamentary language. *RONR (12th ed.), 12:56.*

2. Robert Macho moved the main motion.

   Tom Chauvin moved the primary amendment.

   Dick Byers moved a secondary amendment (way to implement the primary amendment).

   John Jones' amendment should be ruled out of order at this time. It may be offered as a new secondary amendment as it is germane to the primary amendment. However, this cannot be done until the pending secondary amendment ("and that they be reimbursed for the costs from our treasury") is disposed of. John Jones can speak against this pending secondary amendment in the hope that it will be defeated thereby allowing him to propose his secondary amendment.

   Vera Smart, realizing that there is some confusion as to implementation of the main motion and feeling that the main motion will be acceptable, rises to say, "There is confusion as to how to provide for an annual supper meeting. If the amendments are voted down, I am prepared to offer the following substitute amendment that I think will best take care of the situation. I will move 'That the annual meeting be a buffet supper meeting that shall be catered by our local Bon Appetit Caterers.'"

   The amendments are voted down and the substitute motion is offered. The chair then processes the substitute motion by asking if the proponents of the pending main motion ("that the annual meeting be a supper meeting") wish to offer any further amendments to their motion. *RONR (12ᵗʰ ed.),* 12:71. They do not. The chair then states that the debate is now on the substitute motion. It is re-stated if necessary.

Ima Practical moves an amendment to the primary amendment (to substitute): "and that the cost does not exceed $48.00 per attending member." (This is a secondary amendment.)

If seconded, this secondary amendment is open for debate and vote. If adopted the debate is on the substitute motion as amended.

The Chair:	There being no further debate, the question is on the amended substitute. Shall this substitute motion as amended, be substituted for the pending main motion? *(Take vote.)*

If the motion to substitute is adopted, the first proposed main motion is no longer before the assembly. If the motion to substitute is lost, debate and vote is on the first-proposed main motion, which is again open for amendment.

The Chair:	*If it is adopted, the chair then says,* the motion to substitute has been adopted. The main motion now reads "That the annual meeting be a buffet supper meeting that shall be catered by our local Bon Appetit Caterers at a cost not to exceed $48.00 per attending member." The question is on the amended main motion. Are you ready for the question? *(take vote, announce result and action.) RONR (12ᵗʰ ed.),*12:69-90.

Lesson 4: Classification and Vote Requirement of Motions

Lesson Objective:

At the end of the lesson, the student should:

1. Understand and be able to identify main motions, subsidiary motions, privileged motions, incidental motions, and motions that bring a question again before the assembly.

2. Know the various vote requirements for many of the motions covered in the lesson.

Lesson Setup:

1. The student should bring a copy of *RONR (12ᵗʰ ed.)*

2. The students are required to read *RONR (12ᵗʰ ed.)* Chapter III, Description of Motions in All Classifications, RONR (12ᵗʰ ed.), 5:1 – 7:4, prior to the workshop.

3. The workshop leader decides whether the Classification and Vote Requirement Questions are answered one question at a time or as a total assignment. As an option, the leader may assign groups of questions to groups of students. In either case the students report back in a plenary session and discuss the answers.

4. The workshop leader has the answer sheet and should provide copies to all students at the end of the lesson.

Lesson Reference Material:

1. *RONR (12ᵗʰ ed.)*

2. Classification and Vote Requirement Questions (provided)

3. Answers to Classification and Vote Requirement Questions (provided)

Questions on Classification and Vote Requirements:

Determine and classify the following motions include the vote requirement for each. Write and check your answers against *RONR (12th ed.)*. This activity may be done individually, in groups or in a plenary session. **NOTE:** There is no order to the questions below. They are in random order and are from various parts of the book. This simulates how parliamentarians generally receive questions – in a random fashion.

1. I move that debate be closed and the vote taken on this resolution at 3:00 p.m.

2. I move that we vote on the pending motion by ballot.

3. I would like to know if it is in order to speak to that motion.

4. I move that we procure the advantages gained from incorporating this society.

5. I move that we have a rising vote on this matter.

6. I demand that we return to the business of this meeting, which is what we came for.

7. I move that we stop business now in order to hear from our honoured guest, Honourable Mayor Lister.

8. I would like to know if this motion would increase the budget allowance.

9. Since my motion is not well received, I beg leave to recall it.

10. I move that the bylaws be amended to include voting privileges for honorary members.

11. I move that we vote immediately on this motion.

12. I move that we adjourn.

13. I move that we nullify the decision passed at the previous meeting authorizing the treasurer to sign checks without the co-signature of the president.

14. I object to the motion that we give to the press the names of the families who receive aid from us.

15. I move that we take from the table the Emergency Resolution #6 on supporting U.N. Police Action.

16. I move that we consider the motion in two parts: first to raise dues, and second, to expand our membership.

17. I move that the motion to discontinue our affiliations with the national society be thrown out.

18. I move that we confirm by a vote of approval the action taken by the executive board in regard to tax payments.

19. I move that we vote again on the amendment that we hold dinner on Friday instead of Saturday.

20. I move to add that the new rules go into effect at the annual meeting.

21. I move to propose again the motion that we hold our annual dance in April instead of May.

22. I move that when this meeting adjourns, it adjourn to meet Tuesday evening at 8:00 p.m.

23. I move to recommit this resolution for further study.

24. I wish to point out that this motion to refer to a committee is out of order since we have already passed a motion to postpone discussion until the next meeting.

25. The chair has ruled that we vote on this proposition now, without due notice. I do not agree with this decision.

26. I move that we stop all business for 15 minutes.

27. I move that the question be postponed and that we consider it at the next meeting.

28. I move that we lay this resolution on the table in order to take up consideration of the budget.

29. Mr. Chairman, will you please ask the speaker to use the microphone?

30. I move that nominations be closed.

31. I doubt the chair's announcement of the result of that vote.

32. I move that we demand that the national association select its next president from among the members of our local unit.

33. I move that we adjourn at 9:00 p.m.

34. I move to recess for ten minutes.

Answers to Questions on Classification and Vote Requirements (*RONR (12th ed.)*)

1. I move that debate be closed and the vote taken on this resolution at 3:00 p.m.

   Limit or Extend Limit of Debate, Subsidiary motion, requiring a two-thirds vote.

   Must be seconded, is not debatable, and is amendable. ***RONR (12th ed.), 15:1-21.***

   See ***RONR (12th ed.), 15:4,*** for treatment of Limit or Extend Limit of Debate as an incidental main motion.

   The implied motion Previous Question together with the motion to Limit or Extend Limit of Debate is treated as one motion and the vote is two-thirds.

2. I move that we vote on the pending motion by ballot.

   Incidental motion, majority vote. ***RONR (12th ed.), 30:3, t30(#96).***

3. I would like to know if it is in order to speak to that motion.

   Requests: Parliamentary Inquiry, Incidental, no vote. ***RONR (12th ed.), 33:2(4).***

4. I move that we procure the advantages gained from incorporating this society.

   Main Motion, majority vote. ***RONR (12th ed.), 10:1-57.***

5. I move that we have a rising vote on this matter.

   Division of the Assembly, Incidental, no vote. ***RONR (12th ed.), 29:4, 29:6.***

6. I demand that we return to the business of this meeting, which is what we came for.

   Call for Orders of the Day, Privileged, usually no vote. ***RONR (12th ed.), 18:1-11.***

7. I move that we stop business now in order to hear from our honoured guest, Honourable Mayor Lister.

   Suspend the Rules, Incidental, two-thirds vote or unanimous (general) consent. ***RONR (12th ed.), 25:1-20.***

   Lay on the Table, Subsidiary, Majority vote. ***RONR (12th ed.), 17:1-24, 17:3(#7).***

8. I would like to know if this motion would increase the budget allowance.

   Request for Information, Incidental, no vote. **RONR (12th ed.), 33:2(#7), 33:6-10**.

9. Since my motion is not well received, I beg leave to recall it.

   Withdraw, Incidental, no vote if unanimous (general) consent is used. **RONR (12th ed.), 33:11-19**.

10. I move that the bylaws be amended to include voting privileges for honorary members.

   Amend Something Previously Adopted, Motion that Brings a Question Again Before the Assembly, Bylaw amendment, two-thirds vote with previous notice required. **RONR (12th ed.), 35:1-17, 57:1**.

11. I move that we vote immediately on this motion.

   Previous Question, Subsidiary, two-thirds vote. **RONR (12th ed.), 16:1-28**.

12. I move that we adjourn.

   Adjourn, Privileged Motion, majority vote. **RONR (12th ed.), 21:1**, or Main Motion, **majority vote. RONR (12th ed.), 21:6**.

13. I move that we nullify the decision passed at the previous meeting authorizing the treasurer to sign checks without the co-signature of the president.

   Rescind, Incidental Main Motion, two-thirds vote without notice or majority with notice or a majority of the entire membership. **RONR (12th ed.), 3:1-5-13**.

14. I object to the motion that we give to the press the names of the families who receive aid from us.

   Object to Consideration of a Question, Incidental, two-thirds vote (or unanimous consent) against consideration. **RONR (12th ed.), 26:1-9**.

15. I move that we take from the table the Emergency Resolution #6 on supporting U.N. Police Action.

   Take from the Table, Motions That Bring a Question Again Before the Assembly, majority vote. **RONR (12th ed.), 34:1-10**.

16. I move that we consider the motion in two parts: first to raise dues, and second, to expand our membership.

   Division of a Question, Incidental, Usually by unanimous (general) consent. **RONR (12th ed.), 27:1-15**.

17. I move that the motion to discontinue our affiliations with the national society be thrown out.

Postpone Indefinitely, Subsidiary, majority vote. **RONR (12th ed.), 11:1-8**.

18. I move that we confirm by a vote of approval the action taken by the executive board in regard to tax payments.

Ratify, Incidental Main Motion, majority vote. **RONR (12th ed.), 10:52-57**.

19. I move that we vote again on the amendment that we hold dinner on Friday instead of Saturday.

Reconsider, Motions That Bring a Question Again Before the Assembly, Incidental Main Motion, which must be made by one who voted on the prevailing side, majority vote. **RONR (12th ed.), 6:27(5), 37:1-52**.

20. I move to add that the new rules go into effect at the annual meeting.

Proviso, Subsidiary (Amend), or Incidental Motion, majority vote. **RONR (12th ed.), 56:15, 37:1-52**.

21. I move to propose again the motion that we hold our annual dance in April instead of May.

Renew if considered a different question, Main Motion, majority vote. **RONR (12th ed.), 38:1-9**.

22. I move that when this meeting adjourns, it adjourn to meet Tuesday evening at 8:00 p.m.

Fix the Time to Which to Adjourn, Privileged when business pending; majority vote. **RONR (12th ed.), 22:1-20.** Made as a Main Motion; **majority vote. RONR (12th ed.), 22:4**.

23. I move to recommit this resolution for further study.

Refer to a committee, Subsidiary, majority vote. **RONR (12th ed.), 13:1-26**.

24. I wish to point out that this motion to refer to a committee is out of order since we have already passed a motion to postpone discussion until the next meeting.

Point of Order, Incidental, no vote. **RONR (12th ed.), 23:1-21**.

25. The chair has ruled that we vote on this proposition now, without due notice. I do not agree with this decision.

Appeal; Incidental; majority vote or a tie vote to sustain the decision of the chair. **RONR (12th ed.), 24:1-13**.

26. I move that we stop all business for 15 minutes.

    Recess; Privileged if a question is pending, or a Main Motion if no business pending; majority vote. **RONR (12ᵗʰ ed.), 20:1-10**.

27. I move that the question be postponed and that we consider it at the next meeting.

    Postpone to A Certain Time, Subsidiary, majority vote. **RONR (12ᵗʰ ed.), 14:1-22**.

28. I move that we lay this resolution on the table in order to take up consideration of the budget.

    Lay on the Table, Subsidiary, majority vote. **RONR (12ᵗʰ ed.), 17:1-24**.

29. Mr. Chair, will you please ask the speaker to use the microphone?

    Raise a Question of Privilege, Privileged Motion, no vote. **RONR (12ᵗʰ ed.), 19:1-17**.

30. I move that nominations be closed.

    Motion to Close Nominations, Incidental, two-thirds vote or unanimous (general) consent. **RONR (12ᵗʰ ed.), 31:1-7, 46:20**.

31. I doubt the chair's announcement of the result of that vote.

    Division of the Assembly, Incidental, no vote – it is a demand. **RONR (12ᵗʰ ed.), 29:1-8**.

32. I move that we demand that the national association select its next president from among the members of our local unit.

    Dilatory or Out of Order, no vote. **RONR (12ᵗʰ ed.), 39:1-7**.

33. I move that we adjourn at 9:00 p.m.

    Adjourn, Main Motion, majority vote. **RONR (12ᵗʰ ed.), 21:2, 21:6**.

34. I move to recess for ten minutes.

    Recess, Privileged if business pending or main motion if no business pending, majority vote. **RONR (12ᵗʰ ed.), 20:1-10**.

Lesson 5: Motion to Limit or Extend Debate and Previous Question (Close Debate and Vote Immediately)

Lesson Objective:

At the end of the lesson, the student should:

1. Understand the purpose of the subsidiary motions *Limit or Extend the Limits of Debate* and the *Previous Question* (or *Close Debate and Vote Immediately*).

2. Know the characteristics of *Limit or Extend the Limits of Debate* and *Previous Question* (or *Close Debate and Vote Immediately*).

3. Understand the process of handling *Limit or Extend the Limits of Debate* and the *Previous Question* (or *Close Debate and Vote Immediately*) in a presiding situation.

4. Know the various ways or options for limiting debate or extending debate, including its use as a main motion.

Lesson Setup:

1. The student should bring a copy of *RONR (12th ed.)*

2. The Limit or Extend Limits of Debate and Previous Question Summaries are read and discussed prior to doing the exercises. As an option, the relevant sections in *RONR (12th ed.)* may also be read.

3. The students participate in the skit.

4. Questions. The workshop leader decides whether the questions are answered one question at a time or as a total assignment. The workshop leader may prefer to assign groups of questions to small groups of students. In either case the students report back in a plenary session and discuss the answers.

5. Only the workshop leader has the answer sheet but provides copies to all students at the end of the lesson.

Lesson Reference Material:

1. *RONR (12th ed.)*

2. Short introduction to Limit or Extend Limits of Debate and Previous Question (provided)

3. Limit or Extend Limits of Debate and Previous Question Summaries (provided)

4. Skit on the use of Limit or Extend Limits of Debate and Previous Question (provided)

5. Questions on Limit or Extend Limits of Debate and Previous Question (provided)

6. Answers to Questions (5) (provided)

Introduction: Limit or Extend Limits of Debate and Previous Question (Close Debate and Vote Immediately):

At one time in the English Parliament it was considered the right of every member to speak as long and as often as the member liked on any question. Gradually, however, it came to be recognized that a very talkative member, taking advantage of this right, might be infringing on the rights of other members. Moreover, although the word "Parliament" comes from the French verb, "parler," to speak, the ultimate purpose of speaking was to reach a decision – originally on whether to give the King the money he was asking for, but later, as Parliament's power increased, on many other matters. If no limits were placed on debate, it might take too long to reach a decision. As the volume of business increased, ways had to be found to limit debate. Most legislative bodies now place a time limit on members' speeches. For instance, the U.S. House of Representatives has a rule that no member may speak on a question for more than an hour. In the Canadian House of Commons, members' speeches, with certain exceptions, are limited to 40 minutes.

In meetings of ordinary clubs and societies, a rule limiting speeches to an hour or even half an hour would make little sense since business meetings, unlike legislative sessions, often last for only an hour or so. Robert decided that a ten-minute limit would be a good one. He combined this with a rule that each member has a right to speak twice on the same question on the same day (a maximum total of 20 minutes), but is not permitted to make a second speech on the same question as long as any member who has not spoken on that question wishes to do so. ***RONR (12th ed.), 4:25-33, 43:12, 43:35-40*** "Debatability of Motions." Even this time limit seems unduly generous for a short business meeting and, of course, every organization has the right to make its own rule to meet its own needs. *RONR (12th ed.)* 's ten-minute rule applies "in a non-legislative body or organization that has no special rule relating to the length of speeches." ***RONR (12th ed.), 43:8-11.***

(**Note: *AIPSC*** refers to the motion to *Close Debate and Vote Immediately*. ***AIPSC*** does not set a time limit for debate or limit the number of times that a member may speak, and leaves that up to the organization to determine. ***AIPSC*, pp. 21, 65-70, 128.**)

Whether an organization decides to adopt Robert's "ten-minute, two speech" rule or one of its own, there may be occasions when it wants to suspend its general rule on the subject to meet particular circumstances. There are two subsidiary motions that can be adopted on such an occasion; *Limit or Extend the Limits of Debate* is one, the *Previous Question* is the other. Which you will adopt depends on the circumstances. You may have occasion to adopt both during the same debate.

Limit or Extend Limits of Debate Summary

RONR (12ᵗʰ ed.) 15:1-21

The motion to *Limit or Extend Limits of Debate* is the third highest ranking of the subsidiary motions. By means of it, the rules of debate relating to a pending question can be modified in a variety of ways. They may be summarized as follows:

1. The number or length of speeches permitted may be reduced.

2. It may be provided that at a specified later hour or after discussion for a stated length of time, debate shall be closed, and the question put to a vote.

3. More or longer speeches may be allowed than under the general rule.

Standard Descriptive Characteristics governing the subsidiary motion to *Limit or Extend Limits of Debate*: (*RONR (12ᵗʰ ed.)*, 15:5).

1. Takes precedence over all debatable motion. Yields to *Previous Question* and *Lay on the Table,* to all privileged motions, and to all applicable incidental motions.

2. Can be applied to immediately pending debatable motion or to a series of motions.

3. It requires recognition. (Is out of order when another has the floor.)

4. It requires a second.

5. Is not debatable.

6. Is amendable.

7. It requires a two-thirds vote in the affirmative for adoption.

8. It may be reconsidered before the order is exhausted.

If you stop to think about these rules, you will realize that they are, for the most part, based on common sense. For instance, if you want to limit debate on a pending question, you should not waste time discussing whether you should limit it. This argument may not have the same force in the case of extending debate, but if more time is needed to discuss the pending question, you probably shouldn't waste time debating whether it should be granted.

It is logical that the motion should be amendable as to time, for there may be differences of opinion as to the extent to which debate should be modified.

A two-thirds vote in the affirmative is required for adoption because modifying debate deprives members temporarily of certain basic rights. This should not be done unless a large percentage believes that the circumstances warrant it. Even in the case of extending debate, you may be depriving members of certain rights. For instance, if a particular member is granted additional time to speak on a pending question because of the member's special knowledge of it, there may be inadequate time left for other members to express their views. Even if there is a general extension of time applicable to all members, this may deprive a member who wishes to make a motion dealing with another subject of the opportunity to do so.

It is reasonable, too, that the motion to modify debate may be reconsidered even if partially executed. As discussion of the motion to which it has been applied continues, it may become clear that the limitation or extension is no longer necessary or that a further modification is needed. If this occurs, it makes good sense to reconsider it.

The motion to *Limit or Extend Limits of Debate* can be applied to a series of motions as well as to a single one. For instance, if a main motion, an amendment, and a motion to commit were pending, a motion to limit debate on the motion to commit would be in order; so would one to limit debate on all pending questions.

Limit or Extend Limits of Debate as a Main Motion. If a motion to modify debate is made when no business is pending, it is an incidental main motion, not a subsidiary motion. It is important to understand this distinction. For instance, if at the beginning of a meeting it were desired to change the limits of debate for the entire meeting, a motion to accomplish this would be an incidental main motion. Like the subsidiary motion to modify debate, it would require a two-thirds vote in the affirmative for adoption since it deprives members of certain rights. This motion is debatable (main motion).

The Previous Question (Vote Immediately) Summary:

RONR (12th ed.) 16:1-28

If it is considered desirable not just to limit debate, but to stop it altogether, prevent further amendments, and take an immediate vote on the pending question or questions, the way to do so is to move the previous question. This is a technical and rather misleading term which many experts on procedure favor abolishing. The *Previous Question*, which is the second highest ranking of the subsidiary motions, originated in the English Parliament in 1604. Its purpose was to prevent the House from coming to a decision on the subject of debate. The U.S. Congress gradually changed the English previous question into a motion to close debate and vote immediately on the pending question or questions.

The term "close debate" is sometimes proposed as an alternative to the name the "previous question". Traditionalists, however, object to the term on the ground that, to use Lewis Deschler's words, "A motion to close debate does nothing except terminate debate on the main proposition, whereas a motion for the previous question not only ends debate but prevents the offering of amendments or other motions of lesser precedence." *Deschler's Rules of Order,* vii. Alice Sturgis considered "vote immediately" a more accurate and descriptive term. See **AIPSC, pp. 67-70**. There is an even shorter name, "vote now." It expresses in plain and simple English the purpose of the motion traditionally called the previous question. ***RONR (12th ed.)*** continues to use the term "previous question," but follows it in the section heading with this description; "Immediately to close debate and the making of subsidiary motions except the motion to *Lay on the Table.*" ***RONR (12th ed.), 16:1.***

Standard Descriptive Characteristics of *Previous Question*: (*RONR (12th ed.), 16:5*).

1. Takes precedence over all debatable or amendable motions and over *Limit or Extend Limits of Debate.* Yields to *Lay on the Table,* all privileged motions, and all applicable incidental motions.

2. Can be applied to an immediately pending debatable or amendable motion or to a series of such motions.

3. It requires recognition (not in order when another has the floor).

4. It requires a second.

5. Is not debatable.

6. Is not amendable.

7. A two-thirds vote in the affirmative is required for adoption.

8. It may be reconsidered before any vote has been taken under the order but cannot be reconsidered after the order has been partly executed.

If several motions are pending and you wish the assembly to vote immediately on the pending one, you should say:

"I move the previous question."

OR

"I move that we vote immediately."

If you wish the assembly to vote in succession, on all pending questions without further debate on any of them, you should say:

"I move the previous question on all pending questions."

OR

"I move that we vote immediately on all pending questions."

Question! Question! An unfortunate practice has arisen in many deliberative assemblies of calling out "Question! Question!" if a member wants the pending question to be put immediately. This is not a proper way to request an immediate vote. The chair should ignore it or, if the member persists, ask "Do you wish to make a motion to *Vote Immediately*?" or "Is it your intention to move the *Previous Question*?" The member should be required to obtain the floor and make the motion in the proper way.

An alternative way for the chair to handle the matter is to ask the assembly if there is any objection to taking an immediate vote. If there is none, a vote may be taken on the pending question. However, the need for a motion to vote immediately generally arises when a controversial matter is under debate and a small minority wants to continue the discussion. Therefore, it is not highly likely that a request for an immediate vote will carry by unanimous consent.

The accompanying skit is designed to demonstrate the use of the motions to *Limit or Extend Limits of Debate* and the *Previous Question (Vote Immediately)*. It will illustrate how these motions are used and show you the forms they should take.

Skit to Illustrate the Use of the Motions To Limit or Extend Limits of Debate and Previous Question (To close Debate and Vote Immediately)

CAST: The Chair; Members A, B, C, D, E, F, and H. There are references to Member G, but no spoken part is assigned to G.)

Assume that the following motions are pending:

1. A main motion: That our club sponsor a week's skiing holiday in Aspen, Colorado, in January.

2. A primary amendment to strike out "skiing holiday, in Aspen, Colorado" and insert "vacation in Florida."

3. A secondary amendment to strike out "Florida" and insert "Puerto Rico."

Member A: Mr./Madam President.

Chair: Member A.

Member A: We've spent half an hour discussing the advantages and disadvantages of Florida and various locations in Florida. We've defeated a secondary amendment to insert "Fort Lauderdale" before "Florida" in the primary amendment. Now we're expected to discuss another secondary amendment to strike out "Florida" altogether and consider going to Puerto Rico instead. We can't go on like this or we'll never reach a decision. I move that debate on the pending secondary amendment be limited to a total of 10 minutes.

Member B: I second the motion.

Chair: It is moved and seconded to limit debate on the pending secondary amendment to 10 minutes.

Member C: Mr./Madam President.

Chair: For what purpose does the member rise? The motion to limit debate is not debatable.

Member C: I wish to move an amendment to the motion to limit debate, Mr./Madam President.

Chair: A motion to amend would be in order. The chair recognizes Member C.

Member C: I move to amend the motion to limit debate by striking out "10" and inserting "15".

Chair:	Is there a second? (pause – no response). There being no second, the motion to amend the motion to limit debate is not before the assembly. The question is on the motion that we limit debate on the pending secondary amendment to 10 minutes. As this motion requires a two-thirds vote in the affirmative for adoption, the chair will take a rising vote. Those in favor of the motion, please rise ... Be seated. Those opposed, please rise ... Be seated. There are two-thirds in the affirmative and the motion is adopted. Debate on the pending secondary amendment will be limited to 10 minutes. Is there discussion on the secondary amendment?
Member C:	If we have to go in January, and that seems to be the most suitable time for members who are likely to go, Puerto Rico would be a much better location than Florida. It's cold in Florida in January, I know, I've been there at that time of the year.
Member A:	I rise to speak against the proposed secondary amendment. A holiday in Puerto Rico would cost more than one in Florida. I have several travel brochures at home, and I know this is true. January is a bargain month in Florida mainly because it generally is a bit chilly.
Member B:	I move the previous question.
Member D:	I second the motion.
Chair:	The previous question is moved and seconded. Those in favor...
Member C:	Point of Order. We moved to limit debate to 10 minutes. We haven't had 10 minutes debate, so we can't close debate now.
Chair:	Your point of order is not well taken. It is in order to move the previous question after a motion to limit debate has been adopted and before the time limit has expired. Those in favor of ordering the previous question ...
Member E:	Mr./Madam President.
Chair:	For what purpose does the member rise? The immediately pending question is not debatable.
Member E:	I want to ask a question. I don't understand what we're doing. What's this previous question? Are we back to Florida or skiing in Colorado? I thought we had to vote on Puerto Rico.
Chair:	Your question is in order. It is a parliamentary inquiry, which the chair will try to answer. This previous question is the technical name for the motion to close debate, prevent the making of further amendments or other subsidiary motions

except to lay on the table, and to take an immediate vote on the pending question. Thus, we are voting on whether to take an immediate vote on adopting the secondary amendment that, as you say, concerns Puerto Rico.

Member E: Thank you, Mr/Madam President, but I'm still confused, why can't we use language that ordinary people like me can understand?

Chair: Instead of saying "I move the previous question," Member B could have said "I move that we vote immediately." If the term, "previous question" is causing confusion, the chair will put the question in simpler language. Remember though that this motion, by whatever name we call it, requires a two-thirds vote in the affirmative for adoption. The chair will therefore take a rising vote. Those in favor of voting immediately on the secondary amendment to strike out "Florida" and insert "Puerto Rico" please rise ... Be seated. Those opposed, please rise ... Be seated. There are two-thirds in the affirmative and the motion is adopted. We will now vote on the adoption of the secondary amendment. Those in favor of striking out "Florida" and inserting "Puerto Rico" say *aye*. Those opposed, say *no*. The ayes have it and the secondary amendment is adopted. The question is now on the adoption of the primary amendment as amended which reads: To strike out "skiing holiday in Aspen, Colorado," and insert "vacation in Puerto Rico." Is there discussion on this proposed amendment?

Member F: Mr./Madam President.

Chair: Member F.

Member F: Member G has expert knowledge of Puerto Rico as she has spent several winters there. It happens that she has brought some slides along. I think that Member G should be allowed to give a 15-minute illustrated talk on Puerto Rico. Can this be done by unanimous consent?

Chair: It can if no one objects. Is there any objection to Member G's being allowed 15 minutes to tell us ...

Member A: I object. This debate is going to last all night. Anyway, I'm not interested in going to Puerto Rico. I want to go skiing in Colorado.

Chair: There being an objection, we cannot allow Member G 15 minutes to speak by unanimous consent. Do you wish to make a motion on the subject, Member F?

Member F:	Yes, Mr./Madam President, I move that Member G be allowed to give a 15-minute illustrated talk on Puerto Rico as part of this debate.
Member C:	I second the motion.
Chair:	It is moved and seconded to allow Member C to give a 15-minute illustrated talk on Puerto Rico as part of this debate. This is a motion to extend debate. It proposes to allow one member, because of her expertise on the subject, to make a speech of more than 10 minutes. As it may deprive other members of their rights, it requires a two-thirds vote in the affirmative for adoption.
Member E:	Mr./Madam President.
Chair:	Yes, Member E. Have you another question? The chair assumes that you realize that the motion to extend debate is not debatable.
Member E:	Oh, I don't know what's debatable and what isn't. But I thought everyone could speak for 20 minutes. Why do we need a special motion to let Member G speak for 15?
Chair:	According to our parliamentary authority, *RONR (12th ed.),* each member may speak on the same question on the same day for 10 minutes and may speak a second time for 10 minutes after all members who wish to speak on the pending question have had an opportunity to do so. No one may speak for 15 minutes at a time without permission of the assembly.
Member E:	Oh, I see. Thank you, Mr./Madam President. I'm sorry to be so stupid.
Chair:	The question is on allowing Member G to give a 15-minute illustrated talk on Puerto Rico as part of the debate. Those in favor of the motion, please rise ... Be seated. Those opposed, please rise ... Be seated. There are two-thirds in the affirmative and the motion is adopted.
	Member G, would you care now to address the assembly.
NOTE:	Member G's talk follows.
Member D:	Now that Member G has told us so much about Puerto Rico, I'm sure we know without further debate whether we want to go there. I therefore move that we vote immediately on all pending questions.
Member B:	I second the motion.

Chair:	It is moved and seconded that we vote immediately on all pending questions. Those in favor of voting now, please rise ... Be seated. Those opposed, please rise ... Be seated. There are two-thirds in the affirmative and the motion is adopted. We will vote immediately on the proposed amendment to strike out "skiing holiday in Aspen, Colorado" and insert "vacation in Puerto Rico." Those in favor of the amendment, say *aye*. Those opposed say *no*. The ayes have it and the amendment is adopted. The question is now on the main motion as amended which reads: "That our club sponsor a week's vacation in Puerto Rico in January." Those in favor ...
Member E:	Please, Mr./Madam President, I don't understand.
Chair:	What is it now, Member E? (patiently)
Member E:	We've already voted twice to go to Puerto Rico. Do we have to do it a third time?
Chair:	We adopted a secondary amendment to strike out "Florida" in the primary amendment and insert "Puerto Rico". Then we adopted a primary amendment to strike out "skiing holiday in Aspen, Colorado," and insert "vacation in Puerto Rico" in the main motion. It may be that some members of the club don't favor sponsoring a holiday at all. They may have voted to insert "Puerto Rico" because they think it will be easier to defeat a motion to sponsor a vacation in Puerto Rico than one in Florida or Colorado. Therefore, it is essential that we take a vote on the main motion as amended. Do you understand now?
Member E:	Not really, but I'll take your word for it, Mr./Madam President. You seem to know all about parliamentary procedure, which is just great.
Chair:	The question is on the main motion as amended. Those in favor of the motion say *aye*. Those opposed, say *no*. The ayes have it, the motion is adopted, and we will sponsor a vacation in Puerto Rico in January. The travel committee will make preliminary arrangements and report at our next regular meeting. Please let the chair of that committee know if you are likely to be interested in joining this group. If there is no further business, the chair will declare the meeting adjourned. [Pause] There being none, the meeting is adjourned.

****

As the members begin to leave, these comments are heard:

Member A:	I still want to go skiing in Colorado.

Member E: It's all too confusing. I wonder if they do it any differently in Puerto Rico.

Questions on the Motions to Limit or Extend Limits of Debate and Previous Question

Following the lesson and the skit, students may use **RONR (12th ed.)** to research these questions. Twenty-five minutes should be sufficient.

1. What are the Standard Descriptive Characteristics governing the application of the subsidiary motion to *Limit or Extend Limits of Debate*?

2. To which subsidiary motions can "limit" NOT be applied?

3. What are *RONR (12th ed.)*'s rules on limitation of debate in an ordinary meeting?

4. Why are the motions *Limit or Extend Limits of Debate* and *Previous Question* not debatable?

5. Which of the two motions is amendable and why?

6. What are the Standard Descriptive Characteristics governing the application of the motion *Previous Question*?

7. What is the main purpose of *Limit or Extend Limits of Debate* and *Previous Question*?

8. How does the application of *Limit or Extend Limits of Debate* affect pending motions?

9. When is the motion *Limit or Extend Limits of Debate* considered to be exhausted?

10. If the motion *Previous Question* is in order, does it apply to the preamble of a resolution?

11. What happens to the motion *Previous Question* if it is not acted on until the next meeting?

12. What are the forms of *Limit or Extend Limits of Debate*?

13. Can these motions be used in committee?

14. What unfair advantage could a member achieve by moving the *Previous Question* immediately following debate on a motion?

15. What is the motion to limit debate called in the U.S. Senate?

16. Can these motions be reconsidered?

Answers to Questions on the Motions to Limit or Extend Limits of Debate and Previous Question

Students' answers are to be checked against *RONR (12th ed.)*. After each question, a student may read the lesson answer.

1. What are the Standard Descriptive Characteristics governing the application of the subsidiary motion to *Limit or Extend Limits of Debate*?

    a. Takes precedence over all debatable motions.

    b. Can be applied to immediately pending debatable motion, to an entire series of pending debatable motions, or to any consecutive part of such a series beginning with the immediately pending question.

    c. Is out of order when another has the floor.

    d. Must be seconded.

    e. Is not debatable.

    f. Is amendable, but any amendment, like the motion itself, is undebatable.

    g. Requires a two-thirds vote.

    h. An affirmative vote can be reconsidered, without debate, at any time before the order is exhausted.

       RONR (12th ed.), 15:5(8).

2. To which subsidiary motions can "limit" NOT be applied?

    Previous Question and *Lay on the Table*. **RONR (12th ed.), 15:5(2).**

3. What are *RONR (12th ed.)*'s rules on limitation of debate in an ordinary meeting?

    In non-legislative bodies or organizations having no special rules relating to debating time, a member can speak no longer than ten minutes for no more than twice on the same subject on the same day making a total of twenty minutes. The second turn may only be granted when all who wish to speak the first time have had an opportunity to do so. **RONR (12th ed.), 43:8.**

4. Why are the motions *Limit or Extend Limits of Debate* and *Previous Question* not debatable?

    Debate of the three highest-ranking subsidiary motions is not permitted since it would defeat their purpose to stop debate. **RONR (12th ed.), 6:8, 43:37(4-5).**

5. Which of the two motions is amendable and why?

   Limit debate because there may be a desire to modify the extension or limitation proposed. **RONR (12th ed.), 6:7, 15:5(8).**

6. What are the Standard Descriptive Characteristics governing the application of the motion *Previous Question*?

   a.   Takes precedence over all debatable or amendable motions.

   b.   Can be applied to any immediately pending debate or amendable motion or a series.

   c.   Is out of order when another has the floor.

   d.   Must be seconded.

   e.   Is not debatable.

   f.   Is not amendable.

   g.   Requires a two-thirds vote.

   h.   An affirmative vote can be reconsidered before any vote has been taken under the order of the *Previous Question* but cannot be reconsidered after the order has been partly executed.

   RONR (12th ed.), 16:5

7. What is the main purpose of *Limit or Extend Limits of Debate* and *Previous Question*?

   To exercise control of debate on a pending question **RONR (12th ed.), 15:1,** or to bring the assembly to an immediate vote and prevent any further amendments. **RONR (12th ed.), 16:1.**

8. How does the application of *Limit or Extend Limits of Debate* affect pending motions?

   Depends on the nature of the specific provisions. **RONR (12th ed.), 15:6.**

9. When is the motion *Limit or Extend Limits of Debate* considered to be exhausted?

   When all questions on which it has been imposed have been voted on, or the questions have been referred to a committee or postponed indefinitely, or on conclusion of the session. **RONR (12th ed.), 15:18.**

10. If the motion *Previous Question* is in order, does it apply to the preamble of a resolution?

    The order for the motion does not apply to the preamble. **RONR (12th ed.), 16:8.**

11. What happens to the motion *Previous Question* if it is not acted on until the next meeting?

If the interruption of execution of the order for the *Previous Question* occurred by means other than referral and the question comes up again during the same session, the order is still in effect. If the question comes up at a <u>later session</u>, the *Previous Question* is always exhausted. **RONR (12th ed.), 16:12.**

12. What are the forms of *Limit or Extend Limits of Debate*?

    a.   reducing the number of speeches.

    b.   reducing the length of speeches.

    c.   requiring a certain time for closing debate.

    d.   limiting the number of persons who may speak on either side.

    e.   setting a time limit for a particular speaker.

RONR (12th ed.), 15:2, 15:19.

13. Can these motions be used in committee?

No. **RONR (12th ed.), 15:1, 16:4, (see 49:21, Procedure in Small Boards)**

14. What unfair advantage could a member achieve by moving the *Previous Question* immediately following debate on a motion?

By moving the previous question after debating a member may prevent hostile debate or any unfavourable amendments that could be made by opponents.

Robert allows the *Previous Question* to be moved following debate on a motion because when the floor is gained it may be used for any legitimate purpose. **RONR (12th ed.), 42:5.**

It could be agreed upon at the beginning of any debate that such use of the motion *Previous Question* will not be permitted. This can be done by unanimous consent.

(Note: DM, pp. 95-96, and AIPSC, p 26, do not allow it.)

15. What is the motion to limit debate called in the U.S. Senate?

Cloture. **RONR (12th ed.), 16:5n14, footnote (last sentence of first paragraph).**

16. Can these motions be reconsidered?

A negative vote on *Limit or Extend Limits of Debate* may be reconsidered if progress in debate has essentially made it a new question. ***RONR (12th ed.), 15:5(8).***

A negative vote on the *Previous Question* debate may be reconsidered if progress in debate has essentially made it a new question. ***RONR (12th ed.), 16:5(8).***

Lesson 6: Practice in Reference Skills

Lesson Objective:

At the end of the lesson, the student should:

1. Know the layout of the many chapters in *RONR (12th ed.)*.

2. Be able to find more readily specific references in *RONR (12th ed.)*.

Lesson Setup:

1. The student should bring a copy of *RONR (12th ed.)*

2. The workshop leader, using *RONR (12th ed.)*, Table of Contents explains the layout of the book.

3. The workshop leader decides whether the reference questions are answered one question at a time or as a total assignment. As an option, the workshop leader may assign groups of questions to smaller groups of students. In either case the students report back in a plenary session and discuss the answers.

4. Only the workshop leader has the answer sheet but provides copies to all students at the end of the lesson.

Lesson Reference Material:

1. *RONR (12th ed.)*

2. Practice in Reference Skills Questions (provided)

3. Answers to Questions (provided)

Practice in Reference Skills:

Prior to beginning the practice, the workshop leader should take the students through the **Table of Contents of RONR (12ᵗʰ ed.), ix-xxi,** explaining the layout and in particular that dealing with the types of motions. **NOTE:** There is no order to the questions below. They are in random order and are from various parts of the book. This simulates how parliamentarians generally receive questions – in a random fashion.

1. When may two motions be made at one time?

2. What are two unique features of the motion to *Reconsider*?

3. How may differences of opinion regarding rules of order be resolved at a mass meeting?

4. What members may caucus?

5. May the chair put the auditor's report to vote without a motion to do so?

6. When was the requirement that a negative vote be taken introduced?

7. Is debate closed when the chair rises to put the question?

8. Can a meeting be called to order if a quorum is not present?

9. What further action must be taken when the reading of the minutes is "dispensed with?"

10. What verifies the result of the vote?

11. Why is the motion to make a ballot vote unanimous out of order?

12. What are *RONR (12th ed.)* 's suggestions for determining that an amendment is germane?

13. What can a member of a committee do if disagreeing with the committee's report?

14. May members be assessed for funds other than dues?

15. How does the motion to *Create a Blank* make an exception to the rule that only two amendments may be pending at one time?

16. Does *RONR (12th ed.)* require that the presence of a quorum be noted in the minutes?

17. Can any action be adopted without a motion to do so?

18. When is *Adjourn* a privileged motion and when is it a main motion?

19. How can supporting facts contained in a report endanger its adoption?

20. How is continued service of officers ensured?

21. How should a quorum requirement be changed in the bylaws?

Answers to Questions on Practice in Reference Skills:

Prior to beginning the practice, the workshop leader should take the students through the **Table of Contents of RONR (12ᵗʰ ed.), ix-xxi,** explaining the layout and in particular that dealing with the types of motions. **NOTE:** There is no order to the questions below. They are in random order and are from various parts of the book. This simulates how parliamentarians generally receive questions – in a random fashion.

1. When may two motions be made at one time?

    RONR (12ᵗʰ ed.), 25:5. To adopt the motion to *Suspend the Rules* in order to take up a report would obviously require two motions. Suspend the Rules is, in this case an Incidental Main Motion requiring a two-thirds vote and the motion to take up a report is a main motion requiring a majority vote. Put together the motion becomes one motion, but the two-thirds vote is required.

    The general rule is that no member can make two motions at the same time without the consent of the assembly, which may be given by unanimous (general) consent. A member may rise and explain the need to make two motions, one that the club participate in a community program and explain that if this motion is adopted the member is prepared to offer a motion as to how the club may participate.

2. What are two unique features of the motion to *Reconsider*?

    RONR (12ᵗʰ ed.), 37:10 (a-c). Reconsider is American in origin – it was first made a rule in the House of Representatives in 1802. Its purpose is to permit correction of hasty, ill-advised, or erroneous action and to take into account added information or a changed situation. To provide both usefulness and protection against abuse, it has unique characteristics:

    a. The motion may only be made by one who voted on the prevailing side.

    b. The making of the motion is subject to time limits.

    c. The making of this motion has a higher rank than the consideration.

3. How may differences of opinion regarding rules of order be resolved at a mass meeting?

    RONR (12ᵗʰ ed.), 53:8. Since at a mass meeting, there are no bylaws and no adopted parliamentary authority, and often no professional parliamentarian, the rules are assumed to be those of common parliamentary law and differences of opinion can be resolved by citing a recognized parliamentary manual. However, there must be some agreement among the members as to what common law rules are, such as majority decide, decisions are determined by vote, only one may speak at a time. These are the commonly established precedents, among others.

4. What members may caucus?

   RONR (12th ed.), 58:19. All known or admitted member partisans of a particular position on an important issue or in support of a particular candidate may attend a caucus, which is sometimes divided into geographical groupings. They meet to plan strategy toward a desired result within the assembly. The purpose of caucus should be to secure the best informed, most representative, most concerned, and most able group to produce the findings. Caucus means *meeting* and is thought to be political in origin. It has a background of Greek, Roman, Algonquin Indian and pre-American Revolution origins.

5. May the chair put the auditor's report to vote without a motion to do so?

   RONR (12th ed.), 48:25. After the auditor has reported and details of it are presented as required, without waiting, the chair puts the questions on adopting the report. This adoption verifies the work of the treasurer's accounts after which there can be no changes made. Majority vote adopts this assumed motion.

6. When was the requirement that a negative vote be taken introduced?

   RONR (12th ed.), p. xxxiii. This rule was introduced in 1604. **"It is no full Question without the Negative part be put, as well as the affirmative,"** as listed by G. Petyt (1689) in his book *Lex Parliamentaria* – entries from the Journal of The House Of Commons. (ibid., p. 161)

7. Is debate closed when the chair rises to put the question?

   RONR (12th ed.), 43:7. The right of members to debate or introduce secondary motions cannot be cut off by the chair's attempting to put a question to vote so quickly that no members can get the floor. There should be no "gaveling through" on the part of the presiding officer. Debate is not closed when the chair rises to put the vote. If any member, with reasonable promptness, rises and addresses the chair, the member is entitled to the floor even if the chair has announced the result of the vote on the question, that vote is now null and void. No presiding officer may cut off debate precipitately or arbitrarily.

8. Can a meeting be called to order if a quorum is not present?

   RONR (12th ed.), 40:6. If the society's rules require that a meeting be held, the absence of a quorum in no way detracts from the fact that the rules were complied with and the meeting was held – even though it had to adjourn immediately, or fix a time to which to adjourn, or recess to take measures to obtain a quorum. If a quorum cannot be obtained, the chair calls the meeting to order, announces the absence of a quorum, and entertains a motion to adjourn.

9. What further action must be taken when the reading of the minutes is "dispensed with?"

RONR (12th ed.), **48:11.** Minutes may be "dispensed with" by a majority vote, no debate. This means that they are not read at this time but deferred until a later time, such as later in the same day or at the next regular meeting. In this case they are read, corrected, and approved before the reading of the minutes of the immediately previous meeting. Minutes, as the official journal of a society, must be approved and cannot be omitted altogether. A motion to "dispense with the reading of the minutes" is not a request to omit their reading altogether.

10. What verifies the result of the vote?

RONR (12th ed.), **4:43-50.** The chair's announcement of the result of a vote is in three parts: 1) statement of which side "has it", 2) declaration that the motion is adopted or lost, 3) statement indicating the effect of the vote, or ordering its execution, if needed or appropriate. The chair's announcement verifies the result. If there is doubt, the result can be confirmed by a call for *Division of the Assembly*, made by any member without a second or a vote to do so. The chair may also invoke a *Division of the Assembly*. If the result of the vote is still in doubt, the vote can be re-taken or a formal call for a counted vote may be made. This requires a second, a vote and then the vote is taken by actual count. Such a procedure is time consuming and this motion should not be abused.

11. Why is the motion to make a ballot vote unanimous out of order?

RONR (12th ed.), **45:21.** A motion to make unanimous a ballot vote that was not unanimous is out of order. No one can give another's votes away even if it was only one vote. If the motion to make it unanimous is also voted on by ballot, it may be in order, but any member who *openly* votes against declaring the first vote unanimous will thereby reveal that the member did not vote with the prevailing side – and this procedure violates the member's right to secrecy.

12. What are *RONR (12th ed.)* 's suggestions for determining that an amendment is germane?

RONR (12th ed.), **12:16.** To be germane, an amendment must in some way involve the same question that is raised by the motion to which it is applied. It cannot introduce an independent question.

Whenever there is doubt, the chair should submit the amendment's germaneness to the decision of the assembly. Germane means *relevant* or *appropriate*. The amendment can even be hostile to the motion to which it is applied.

13. What can a member of a committee do if disagreeing with the committee's report?

    RONR (12th ed.), 51:64-65. *Formal Expression of Minority View* is *RONR (12th ed.)* 's term for a minority report. It comes from those committee members who do not concur with all that is contained in a report and the assembly usually permits this request, by unanimous (general) consent. *RONR (12th ed.)* considers this permission a privilege, not a right since the appointment of the committee implies that the assembly is interested in the findings of the majority of its members and that no society can be compelled to take the time to hear a report that it does not want to hear. (Note that ***AIPSC,*** p. **203,** believes that a minority has a right to report its views.)

14. May members be assessed for funds other than dues?

    RONR (12th ed.), 56:19. Members cannot be assessed any additional payments aside from their dues unless this is provided for in the bylaws.

15. How does the motion to *Create a Blank* make an exception to the rule that only two amendments may be pending at one time?

    RONR (12th ed.), 12:92. Although not a form of amendment of itself, it is a clearly related device by which an unlimited number of alternative choices for specifications in a main motion or primary amendment can be pending at the same time. It permits an exception to the rule that there can be only two amendments pending at the same time (a primary and a secondary amendment).

16. Does *RONR (12th ed.)* require that the presence of a quorum be noted in the minutes?

    RONR (12th ed.), 47:7, 3:15, 48:4(4). *RONR (12th ed.)* makes no mention of it, but it is good practice to do so. ***RONR (12th ed.), 40:11,*** states that it is the duty of the presiding officer to determine that a quorum is present although the presiding officer need not announce it. If the court ever impounds minutes during some lawsuit, the fact that a quorum was noted as present may have a very important bearing on the case. (Note that ***AIPSC, pp. 291, 294,*** includes in minutes that a quorum is or is not present.)

17. Can any action be adopted without a motion to do so?

RONR (12th ed.), **4:58-61.** Adopting a motion where there is obviously no opposition and where the motion is of relative unimportance, it may be done without going through all the steps of a formal motion. To protect any possible minority, however, the chair states "If there is no objection ..." and if there is, the chair always puts the motion to vote. Otherwise the chair declares the motion is adopted by unanimous (general) consent. Unanimous consent, although the preferred term in *RONR (12th ed.)*, may be a poor term to use; there is no proof that it is unanimous, just that no one voted no. This may be because of apathy to the motion or because the member thought that voting "no" would be useless. In other words, some might have abstained. (Note that **AIPSC,** p. **148,** prefers the term "general consent.")

Motions that are accepted without a formal motion are "implied" or "assumed" motions.

18. When is *Adjourn* a privileged motion and when is it a main motion?

   RONR (12th ed.), **21:1-20.** The motion to *Adjourn* is privileged when its intent is to close the meeting without any specified time for meeting again. It means that the meeting is to be closed immediately, but under provisions where it will not dissolve the assembly permanently. No society should be forced to continue a meeting when it wants to go home. This motion has high privilege and it is not debatable or amendable. It may be privileged when no business is pending and it is privileged when business is pending. The privileged form of *Adjourn* yields only to *Fix the Time to Which to Adjourn*.

   RONR (12th ed.), **21:3.** The motion to *Adjourn* is a main motion when it sets a future time to meet, when a time for adjournment has been pre-established, or when the motion would dissolve the assembly. It is out of order when any business is pending. It is debatable and amendable. Majority vote carries both forms of *Adjourn*.

19. How can supporting facts contained in a report endanger its adoption?

   RONR (12th ed.), **51:6.** When recommendations are being considered, the reasons for their support can be better expressed in the debate. The inclusion of supporting facts or reasoning in a report proposing certain action may tend to work against the taking of that action. Some members who might otherwise have been willing to accept the proposals may be led to vote against them if they disagree with the factual background as reported or the reasoning of the reporting body. This also applies to the preamble in a resolution when too many arguments are presented.

20. How is continued service of officers ensured?

>   ***RONR (12th ed.), 56:28-30, 62:16***. To ensure the continued services of officers in the event of any emergency or failure to obtain a nominee, it is well to provide in the bylaws that "officers shall hold office for a term of _____ year(s) or (or "and") until their successors are elected."

>   The unqualified term of "_____ years" should be avoided because at the end of that time there would be no officers if new ones had not been elected. If bylaws provide that officers shall serve "for _____ years *or* until their successors are elected," the election of the officer in question can be rescinded and a successor thereafter be elected for the remainder of the term.

>   The vote required for removing the offender from office in such a case is the same as for any other motion to rescind.

>   ***RONR (12th ed.), 62:16***. "If, however, the bylaws provide that officers shall serve *only* a fixed term, such as 'for two years' (which is not a recommended wording; see *RONR (12th ed.),* 56:27-30), or if they provide that officers shall serve 'for _____ years *and* until their successors are elected,' an officer can be removed only for cause—that is, neglect of duty in office or misconduct—in accordance with the procedures described in **63;** that is, an investigating committee must be appointed, charges must be preferred, and a formal trial must be held."

21. How should a quorum requirement be changed in the bylaws?

>   ***RONR (12th ed.), 40:4***. The rule to strike out a quorum requirement should not be struck out first, because then the quorum requirement is instantly a majority of the membership. Strike out and insert the new provision must be made and voted on as one question.

Lesson 7: Decorum

Lesson Objective:

At the end of the lesson, the student should:

1. Be able to analyse a given parliamentary situation and determine how the presiding officer or others should respond to the parliamentary situation.

2. Be knowledgeable of proper decorum and rules of debate in a deliberative assembly.

Lesson Setup:

1. The student should bring a copy of *RONR (12th ed.)*.

2. Some students are assigned to read the script[1] for **Section A,** Exercise 1. At the end of the first reading all students write what they believe to be the most accurate and suitable reply or statement for the last character in the script. They may use *RONR (12th ed.)* and cite references.

3. The students discuss the answers to exercise 1 prior to the workshop leader giving the preferred answer.

4. The students then take up the other exercises in turn. The workshop leader should rotate the reading of the scripts amongst the students.

5. Only the workshop leader has the answer sheet but provides copies to all students at the end of the lesson.

Lesson Reference Material:

1. *RONR (12th ed.)*

2. *Parliamentary Law,* Henry M. Robert, 1923 Edition (2001 reprint)

3. Section A - 9 exercise scripts (provided)

4. Section B - Answers to exercise scripts (provided)

---

[1] The cast of characters in the scripts include:

Narrator	Chairman
Member A	Member B

Exercise 1

NARRATOR: Carefully notice the setting and the script that follows. The setting is a meeting of the Longjohn Manufacturers Association. During the proceedings a member makes a motion "to change the trademark of the Longjohn Manufacturers Association and adopt a new trademark as designed by John Mark Associates, Inc." and the motion is seconded. However, it is similar to a motion adopted previously by the convention in the morning meeting.

MEMBER A: Mr./Madam Chair.

CHAIR: Member A.

MEMBER A: I rise to speak in favor of the motion to change our trademark design. It has the same pictures of oranges, grapes, etc. that is found in the "Fruit of the Loom" trademark used by another association of competitors and the two are similar. I feel ...

MEMBER B: (interrupts Member A) Point of Order, Mr./Madam Chairman!

CHAIR: Please state your point.

MEMBER B: The motion is out of order. It is an improper motion because it deals practically with the same question as a motion adopted this morning; that is, the association will continue to use the same labels, designs, and promotions that were used last year in the sale of Longjohn underwear.

CHAIR: The chair rules the pending motion is not the same as the question considered in the morning meeting, and the pending motion is in order. Member A, you have the floor.

MEMBER A: Mr./Madam Chairman, I resent the interruption of the member and feel that it is a breach of courtesy to interrupt somebody when they are speaking. I mean, I wouldn't do anything like that.

NARRATOR: Each member of the workshop will now write what would be the most correct and suitable response from the chair. What would you have the chair say? (See Section B, Exercise 1)

Exercise 2

NARRATOR: It is the business meeting of the local Lions Club; the chair calls the club to order and has just recognized the secretary for the reading of the minutes. However, just as the secretary is about to read the minutes the following event happens.

MEMBER A: (leaning over and whispering loudly and in a disturbing manner) "Bill, can you get two tickets to the Jets-Dolphin game?"

MEMBER B: (Responding in like manner) "Sure Joe, there's a fellow over on Second Street I know who ..."

NARRATOR: The chair interrupts Member B because the assembly is being disturbed, but just how does the chair handle this kind of situation? Write your response of the chair. (See Section B, Exercise 2)

Exercise 3

NARRATOR: The Lazy Daisy Garden Club is having its monthly meeting and the chair has permitted discussion concerning the planting of shrubbery and flowers around the flagpole in the court square. Now the chair says:

CHAIR: The club is considering a subject pro and con without a motion, and the chair entertains a motion proposing some definite action.

MEMBER A: Mr./Madam Chairman.

CHAIR: Member A has the floor.

MEMBER A: I move that we allocate $500.00 for use by the beautification committee as it deems proper for the landscaping of the immediate grounds about the flagpole on the court square. Mr. Chairman, I wish to speak to the motion.

MEMBER B: I second the motion.

CHAIR: It is moved and seconded to allocate $500.00 for use by the beautification committee as it deems proper for the landscaping of the immediate grounds about the flagpole on the court square. Mr. A has the floor.

MEMBER A: Although I made the motion in response to the request of the chair, I am not in favor of spending our money and energies on the court grounds for two reasons. For one reason, every dog and town drunk uses ...

MEMBER B: (interrupts Member A) Point of Order, Mr./Madam Chairman.

CHAIR: Please state your point.

MEMBER B: My friend is speaking against his own motion, and this is contrary to the rules of decorum in debate. I believe ...

MEMBER A: (interrupts Member B) Why, whata you mean? Of course, I can speak against my own motion. Why not? It is my motion and it's still a free country – I think.

NARRATOR: What is happening here? What should be the response of the chair in a situation like this? Write the chair's response. (See Section B, Exercise 3)

Exercise 4

NARRATOR:	It is the regular city council meeting in Redhole, Minnesota. Member A has the floor and is speaking to the pending motion.
MEMBER A:	It is easy to see why the city manager made this motion and why the manager wants the city to extend corporate limits to include Everbad community. The manager has purchased surrounding properties there and hopes to make a killing by increasing land values with this proposal.
MEMBER B:	Mr./Madam Chairman, I rise to a point of order.
CHAIR:	Please state your point.
NARRATOR:	What is the rule of decorum in debate that Member B is going to bring to the attention of the council? How is Member B going to word it? Write your answer. (See Section B, Exercise 4)

Exercise 5

NARRATOR: The Bugle Baptist Church of Fox Trot, Virginia, is having its regular monthly business meeting and the church is debating the motion to build a new house for the coming minister. One of the older members, saintly and highly respected, has the floor and is speaking.

MEMBER A: I don't see the need for us to build a new house for the preacher and to spend all that money. The preacher's home we have now is good enough. It is a better place than Gracie and I had when we started out. We lived in a cabin up the Laurel Fork Road during the winter of '77. It was so cold that you had to take a fellow's words inside to the fire to thaw so you could hear what he was saying. I remember Ole Blue – everybody knows my dog, Ole Blue, she ...

NARRATOR: The chair interrupts Member A and it is easy to see why, but how is one to handle this problem of decorum without hurting the old gentleman's feelings or offending the congregation? (See Section B, Exercise 5)

Exercise 6

NARRATOR:	It is the meeting of the Harper Valley PTA, and there is an important, controversial motion pending before the group. One member has just made an effective speech in support of the motion, but other members seem reluctant and hesitate to speak against the motion. The chair speaks:
CHAIR:	We have just heard one viewpoint; now let's hear from the other side.
MEMBER A:	Mr./Madam Chairman! Point of Order!
CHAIR:	Please state your point.
MEMBER A:	I am surprised that the chair would promote controversy in our PTA by calling for people to take sides. The chair should be completely non-partisan.
NARRATOR:	Is the chair guilty of being partisan? Is the chair guilty of improper behavior? What would be the response that you would have the chair give to Member A? (See Section B, Exercise 6)

Exercise 7

NARRATOR: There is considerable tension and heated discussion in the annual meeting of a large group of stockholders. A board member has moved to borrow $15 million to purchase the inventory of a bankrupt company, and members are speaking emotionally. We notice it as we hear Member A.

MEMBER A: There is no need for our company to have Joe Thomas on our board of directors if he is going to come up with ideas as crazy as this one. The action he proposes betrays the financial stability of the company. Thomas did the same thing three years ago concerning the merger with the Rubberduck Tub Co. The merger has brought us financial liabilities far beyond the assets and skills of the company. I tried my best to get stockholders to see the foolishness of this merger. It has ...

NARRATOR: The chair interrupts Member A. Write your lines for the chair. (See Section B, Exercise 7)

Exercise 8

NARRATOR:	It is the annual convention of the Congress of American Teacher Societies, better known as the CATS. There has developed a group of teachers within the CATS who have labeled themselves: Reformed American Teacher Societies, known as the RATS. It seems the RATS are philosophically opposed to the policies and programs promoted by the executive committee of the CATS, and the RATS now represent a conservative movement among the CATS. The RATS have organized a caucus and have distributed materials among the delegates during the convention. The copied materials list amendments to be made by the RATS to committee reports and recommendations under the control of the executive committee. More importantly, the RATS have distributed materials promoting the nomination and election of certain members of their number as officers of the CATS. The convention has arrived in its agenda to the time for the election of officers. Let's get in on the happenings.
MEMBER A:	Mr./Madam Chairman, I am Member A, delegate from Rabbit-squat, Kansas.
CHAIR:	Member A is recognized.
MEMBER A:	Mr. Chairman, I raise a question of decorum. I am most disturbed to learn of a well-organized group of self-labeled conservatives known as the RATS at this annual meeting. This is a new development among the CATS, and it is regrettable. Formation of rump groups breeds division, and they compromise the basic unity that has been one of the cherished hallmarks of the CATS. I do not believe that the circulation of materials by the RATS in which they have outlined motions to be presented, and champion certain candidates for office, can possibly be good for the cause of the CATS. I believe this goes too far toward the use of caucus approach in politics, and it tends to result in an unwholesome polarization of our CATS fellowship. It has not been our custom to politic for office. We have never made the election of our officers a political contest. Mr. Chairman, I believe the action has been in poor taste and I ask the chairman to rule on the decorum of these proceedings just described.
NARRATOR:	What is the chair to say? Is the procedure described above a matter of decorum? Has anything been done contrary to rules? Or is Member A expressing resentment

to those who do not go along with the executive committee? Is Member A trying to suppress the minority? (See Section B, Exercise 8)

Exercise 9

NARRATOR: The platform committee of about 40 people is meeting to draw up a policy statement of the state's Young Voters Political Convention. The debate is on the resolution to support Amendment #5 to the national bylaws, but there is strong opposition. Member A has the floor.

MEMBER A: Some of you are opposed to Amendment #5, but you don't know what the amendment even contains. You have never read it, yet you are against it. How can you say you are fair when you deny equality for all Americans? Bigots! You are marble-headed dummies! You don't know the difference between a jackrabbit and a jackass! You are ...

NARRATOR: Just what is to be done in this situation? What should be the action of the chair? (See Section B, Exercise 9)

The following are possible replies and statements related to the circumstances of the script. The workshop leader acts as the narrator who may ask each student to share their responses, and afterward may read the following to the group.

Exercise 1

NARRATOR: Explanations may be needed before the chair's response is given; however, each member will provide only the lines for the character in the script that circumstances in the drama would ordinarily permit. *RONR (12ᵗʰ ed.)* states that when a member has been assigned the floor and has begun to speak, the member cannot be interrupted by another member. **RONR (12ᵗʰ ed.), 42:18.** *RONR (12ᵗʰ ed.)* also recognizes exceptions and circumstances that do justify or allow interruption of a speaker. These exceptions are given in **RONR (12ᵗʰ ed.), 42:18(c)**, and one of these exceptions is for the purpose of making a point of order. Turn to these pages and read these exceptions. See also, **RONR (12ᵗʰ ed.), 23:3,** and read "It is the right of every member who notices a breach of the rules to insist on their enforcement." When a point of order is made, the speaker is to be seated or steps back slightly while the chair makes a ruling. The speaker may later regain the right to the floor. Perhaps the chair could respond in the following manner: "It is not considered a breach of decorum or an act of discourtesy to interrupt a speaker with a legitimate point of order. The member has the right to interrupt in these circumstances. Member A has the floor." Is the chair's ruling that the motion is in order correct?

Exercise 2

NARRATOR: The presiding officer is not to permit members to disturb the assembly. **RONR (12ᵗʰ ed.), 43:28, 47:7(6).** "If the assembly is disorderly, in nine cases out of ten it is the fault of the presiding officer, just as it is the fault of the company commander if there is a lack of discipline in a company of soldiers." Henry M. Robert, *Parliamentary Law, p.* 302. The chair must use tact and common sense and must keep order in a way that is not offensive or harsh. There are different ways the chair might handle this situation. Before the secretary begins to read the minutes, the chair could stand and simply look at the disturbers and this will usually bring order (it is an old trick used by teachers). The chair could rise, gently rap the gavel, and without looking at the culprits, speak in a calm but firm voice: "All members will kindly come to order and give their attention to the reading of the record. The chair is waiting for members to come to order."

Exercise 3
NARRATOR:

It is necessary for the chair to intervene here not only to respond to the point of order but to maintain order. A member may not speak against a motion made by the member; it would permit procedure contrary to good faith. If the member is not in favor of the motion, the member may seek to withdraw it or simply not speak at all. ***RONR (12th ed.), 43:25.*** It is also true that the chair must insist upon the proper procedure of all members securing the floor before they speak and that they address all remarks to the chair; otherwise the chair cannot maintain dignity and order in the assembly. ***RONR (12th ed.), 43:22, 4:30, 42:2.*** The chair says: "Members will please come to order. Thank you. Member B, your point is well taken. It is contrary to the rules of decorum for a member to speak against the member's own motion. Member A, you may request to withdraw your motion, or you may be seated. The chair also reminds all members to secure the floor in proper fashion before speaking. The chair cannot be tolerant at this point."

Exercise 4
NARRATOR:

Member B might respond as follows:
"Mr./Madam Chairman, it is contrary to the standards of propriety in ***Robert's Rules of Order Newly Revised, 12ed. 4:30,*** to attack or question the motives of another member in debate. We should address the issues and avoid personalities."

Exercise 5
NARRATOR:

It is easy to see that Member A is not speaking to the issue, and *RONR (12th ed.)* states that one is to confine one's remarks to the merits of the pending question. ***RONR (12th ed.), 43:20.*** The gentleman's remarks are not germane to the subject. The chair could interrupt the gentleman and speaking gently say, "Kindly address your remarks to the issue of building a house for the new minister. It is in the interests of saving our time."

(Alice Sturgis, in her book, *Learning Parliamentary Procedure, pp.* 65-66, states,

"The most important principle governing discussion and debate is that it must be relevant to the subject before the assembly. Any member who has the floor during discussion has been given it for the purpose of discussing the pending question. If he departs from the subject, he is out of order.")

Exercise 6
NARRATOR: This should not be an occasion for the chair to take offense. A point of order is not grounds for an officer or member to be offended or to be intimidated. **RONR (12th ed.), 23:1, 23:3.** While it is true that the chair is to remain impartial and as objective as possible, the chair's effort to stimulate expression of opposing views is a constructive role for the chair. This would be more necessary in a time of pending controversial questions. The chair would respond accordingly. "Sir, the chair is not in violation of the rule of decorum or is the chair guilty of expressing an opposing view to the question by calling for opposing views. The chair wishes to encourage those of contrary views or opinions to express themselves here and now on this important subject. By seeking to stimulate participation, the chair does not support nor oppose the motion."

(Alice Sturgis states in *Learning Parliamentary Procedure, p.* 61, "It is one of the duties of the presiding officer to guide and stimulate discussion in such a manner that it will arouse the interest of the members and cause them to participate. A capable presiding officer will draw out the ideas and reactions of individual members. He will see to it that there are opportunities to speak and will encourage members to use those opportunities. He will seek to create a climate which is favorable to free, frank and thoughtful discussion; an atmosphere in which members will find every encouragement to express their opinions.")

Exercise 7
NARRATOR: There is more than one violation of parliamentary decorum in this exercise. Member A is attacking a personality, which is not to be done in debate. Member A is also speaking and calling a member by name, as well as speaking in opposition to action that the company

had taken previously, not to the pending question, and this is not in order. *RONR (12th ed.)*, **43:20-24.** The member's remarks must be confined to the merits of the pending question. *RONR (12th ed.)*, **43:20.** The chair could interrupt as tactfully as possible and say, "The member will speak only to the motion that is pending and will not attack any personality, only the issue currently under discussion."

Exercise 8
NARRATOR:

Here is an example that reveals the weakness of procedure based on custom instead of written law. If an assembly wishes to adopt standards of decorum that are not covered by its parliamentary authority, the standard should be included in the special or standing rules of the society. In a convention these additional rules of decorum should be adopted at the time of the rules committee report. A society that proceeds on custom requires members of greater longevity in membership and in service to become authoritative sources to pass on to others the interpretation and application of the customs. This tends to create two groups within the society; with a tendency to divide. The assembly will then have those older members who know and accept the custom – telling the younger group, "This is the way we have always done it." The RATS have not done anything contrary to *RONR (12th ed.)*. *RONR (12th ed.)* recognizes the need of caucus and its organization. *RONR (12th ed.)*, **52:28, 58:19-22.** For a group to meet and plan strategy toward a desired result on the part of convention members is well within their rights. With no rule to the contrary, the RATS are within their rights to promote actively the candidates of their choice, and they have not violated parliamentary law by copying and distributing materials among the delegates. The chair responds, "The chair is not aware of any violation of decorum or breach of parliamentary law in the activity just described. However, the chair will be happy to recognize any specific point of order. If the assembly does not wish the distribution of materials advocating and promoting the election of members to office, then specific rules of order and decorum should be adopted as special rules of orders." (This would have to be done at the next convention as it is obviously too late to do this at the current convention.)

Exercise 9

NARRATOR: The speaker is way out of line and the anger shown only serves to anger other hearers in return. The chair cannot permit such language or behavior. If "opprobrious epithets or offensive language" is used by a speaker, the chair may take steps toward withdrawal of the words by the speaker or securing an apology. ***RONR (12ᵗʰ ed.), 43:20-21.*** The place of appropriate humor on the part of the chair can be as effective as a firm rebuke. Of course, gross profanity cannot be tolerated, but it is the high pitch of emotionalism that is far more dangerous to the welfare of the society. The calming influence of good humor and a chairman who can keep cool can bring warmth and harmony to an assembly caught in cold tension and hot anger. For example, when everybody seems to be clamoring to secure the floor and there is considerable confusion, the chair could say, "I am reminded of two horses pulling a wagon, they do a better job when they have just one tongue between them. The chair will recognize only one tongue at a time." In the exercise here, the chair might say (interrupting the speaker), "My friend, you'll catch more flies with honey than you will with vinegar. Let's not get emotional and use disrespectful language."

(See Henry M. Robert's *Parliamentary Law,* p.149, for a more complete discussion of this situation. If the language is grossly foul and profane, the chair may ask the speaker to be seated, and there can be steps toward censure. The attitude of society, however, is quite different today than it was at the writing of *Parliamentary Law,* and the social climate is far more tolerant.)

Lessons 8 and 9: Bylaws

Lesson Objective:

At the end of the lesson, the student should:

1. Be able to name the different classes of rules an organization may adopt and should understand the relationships and order of precedence between them, including the corporate charter.

2. Understand the purpose of rules and their structure.

3. Be able to name the different sections of the standard bylaws recommended by *RONR (12th ed.)*.

4. Understand the content required in the standard bylaws under *RONR (12th ed.)*.

5. Be able to write a simple set of bylaws for an organization.

6. Be able to analyse a set of bylaws for structure, wording, accuracy and content.

Lesson Setup:

1. Students bring to the meeting:

   - A copy of *RONR (12th ed.)*

   - A copy of the bylaws of an ordinary organization, or

   - A copy of the bylaws of an incorporated organization, or

   - A copy of the bylaws of an organization that has a parent organization.

The workshop leader and students discuss **RONR (12th ed.), 21:1-25,** to understand how the bylaws relate to other rules of a society and in particular the order of precedence of the rules.

Purpose of rules – establish basic structure, manner of operation and rules of procedure.

- Classes of rules – some more difficult to change or suspend than others.

- Restriction – conform to parliamentary law and not in conflict with existing rules or rules of higher order (parent body or applicable procedural rules contained in national, state, or local law).

- Types of rules – corporate charter; constitution and/or bylaws; special rules of order; rules of order; standing rules.

The workshop leader distributes the "Summary of *RONR (12th ed.),* Chapter XVIII Bylaws" which is provided. and discusses in detail each section of the chapter. This is to be done in an interactive manner by probing the students and taking questions as they arise.

The students then proceed to construct a simple set of bylaws for a local organization. This may be done in teams or as a group. The teams present the results of their work.

Note: The above exercises will suffice for the first part of the lesson.

Now that the students understand how a set of bylaws should be constructed and why, the students can now evaluate bylaws of other organizations.

The group is allowed about twenty to thirty minutes to evaluate the bylaws that they brought with them. Each student is then given an opportunity to discuss their evaluation with the entire group.

- Are they well worded?

- Are they properly punctuated?

- Are they correctly aligned for ease of reference?

- Are all necessary provisions included?

- Are unnecessary provisions excluded?

The students should provide good and poor examples of structure, wording, accuracy, or content of bylaws.

a. Using a sample of bylaws of an organization established by corporate charter, point out the relationship of bylaws to the corporate charter.

b. Using a sample of bylaws of an organization having a parent organization, point out the relationship among bylaws of each level of the organization.

The article containing the parliamentary authority in the bylaws of such an organization may include " … and in which they are not inconsistent with these bylaws, the bylaws of the parent organization, and any special rules of order."

In summary, read the following aloud to the group:

It is important to bear in mind that the bylaws of every society are unique – they establish the purpose and organization of the society they serve, and reflect the particular needs, the values, the strengths, and the expertise of those individuals who make up the society.

There are, however, basic principles – provisions – which parliamentary law and common sense tell us should be a part of every set of bylaws. It is this basic structure that we deal with in this lesson, and it is this basic structure upon which every set of bylaws should be built.

Lesson Reference Material:

1. *RONR (12th ed.)*

2. Bylaws from different types of organizations, including a local organization, an organization that is incorporated, and an organization with a parent organization

3. Summary of *RONR (12th ed.)* Chapter XVIII Bylaws (provided)

Summary of *RONR (12th ed.)* Chapter XVIII Bylaws:

A. Importance. RONR (12th ed.), 56:1-2
Defines the rights, powers, and duties of members and of the assembly.

B. Content. RONR (12th ed.), 56:16
1. No more restrictive or more detailed than necessary.

2. Clarity and precision in word choice, sentence structure and punctuation.

3. Each sentence written so that it is impossible to quote out of context. (Clear without reference elsewhere, or it should be worded to compel the reader to refer elsewhere.)

4. Provisions of temporary nature not included in body. **RONR (12th ed.), 57:17**

ARTICLE I: Name. RONR (12th ed.), 56:17
Full, exact, and properly punctuated name – affiliated with (if such be the case). (May omit this article in incorporated societies or those with separate constitution.)

ARTICLE II: Object. RONR (12th ed.), 56:18
Express concisely, in one sentence, if possible. General in application since it sets bounds for introduction of business. (May omit this article in incorporated societies or those with separate constitution.)

ARTICLE III: Members. RONR (12th ed.), 56:19-22
Section 1.   Composition – classes of members (includes rights and/or limitations of each).

      a. Active

      b. Associate

      c. Life

      d. Honorary (RONR (12th ed.), 56:21)

Section 2.   Eligibility or qualification

      a. Requirements (attendance and participation required only if stated in bylaws).

      b. Method of application, acceptance.

      c. Method of removal, reinstatement.

      d. Method of resignation.

Section 3.   Dues and fees (If complex, Finances may be separate article). A specific amount or how established (assessment above dues only if stated in bylaws).

      a. Date(s) payable.

      b. Procedure if delinquent (loss of voting rights if in arrears in payment only if stated in bylaws).

      c. A date on which members will be dropped for non-payment of dues.

ARTICLE IV: Officers. RONR (12th ed.), 56:23-32

Section 1.   List in order of rank. Include officers, directors, and honorary officers and directors.

      a. How elected or appointed.

      b. Length of term (use the phrase "shall hold office for a term of ____ year(s) and until their successors are elected" to assure continuity.) (If "or until" is used an officer can be removed from office by a motion to rescind; if "and until" is used, removal requires investigation, preferred charges, formal trial, etc.)

      c. Limitation of number of consecutive terms.

      d. Eligibility.

      e. Vacancies – method of filling (in office of president, filled by vice-president in order of rank, each vice-president moving forward, and vacancy is filled in lowest ranking vice-presidency, unless bylaws provide otherwise).

Section 2.   Duties of officers and directors. General statement: "Officers shall perform the duties prescribed by these bylaws and by the parliamentary authority adopted by the society." (May be separate article if duties extraordinary.)

      a. President

b. Separate paragraph for each officer.

c. List all duties or add statement for each officer, "and shall perform such other duties as prescribed by these bylaws and by the parliamentary authority adopted by the society"; (omission may imply it is not required and that only the listed duties may be performed).

Section 3.   Nomination (may be separate article with election – recommended).

a. Method of nomination – nominating committee, by petition, from floor, or combination.

b. (If by nominating committee) Method of selection, duties, time frame (if report of nominating committee limited to one candidate for each office, must be so stated).

Section 4.   Election (may be separate article with nomination recommended).

a. Prescribe election by ballot.

b. Dispense with ballot when only one candidate for each office. (Chair can then take voice vote or can declare the nominee elected – sometimes called "acclamation." This provision deprives members of the opportunity for "write-in" voting.)

c. Majority vote required to elect (majority – more than half of votes cast by legal voters which includes illegal ballots). RONR (12th ed.), 44:1. If election by mail, plurality or preferential is preferred, it must be provided for in the bylaws. **RONR (12th ed.), 45:57-61 (by mail); RONR (12th ed.), 44:11 (plurality); RONR (12th ed.). 45:62-69 (preferential voting).**

ARTICLE V: Meetings. RONR (12th ed.), 56:33-38

Section 1.   Regular meetings

Fix day (not time). Allow for change in unusual circumstances.

Section 2.   Provide for annual meeting – for elections and reports.

Section 3.   Provide for special meetings – by whom called and restrictions of business.

Section 4.   Quorum – realistic number of members who may be expected to attend.

ARTICLE VI: Executive Board. (Board of Directors or other title) RONR (12th ed.), 56:39-43

Section 1.   Composition – usually officers and directors.

Section 2.   Powers.

Section 3.   Rules relating to business – when and how often will meet, special meetings, quorum.

(Executive Committee, RONR (12th ed.), 56:40, if applicable, may be separate article, including composition, powers, and rules of conduct.)

ARTICLE VII: Committees. RONR (12th ed.), 56:44-48
Section 1.   Standing Committees

Name, composition, manner of selection, duties of each, in separate sections.

Section 2.   Provision for additional standing committees.

Section 3.   Provision for special committees.

Section 4.   President *ex officio* member of all committees, except nominating committee.

ARTICLE VIII: Parliamentary Authority. RONR (12th ed.), 56:49
One sentence as in reference above.

ARTICLE IX: Amendment of Bylaws. RONR (12th ed.), 56:50-57
Procedure for amendment requiring at least advance notice (and how given) and two-thirds vote.

Important Points About Bylaws:
1. Know which copy of the bylaws is current!

2. Under title of bylaws or at end, include address of society and date of adoption of those bylaws.

3. "Shall" is mandatory.

4. "May" is permissive.

5. A vote of "____ % of the members" requires, as it says, a percentage of the entire membership (present or absent). (Very difficult to get in most societies.)

6. "A ____ % vote" refers to a percentage of those members present and voting. (More reasonable.)

Lesson 10: Exceptions to the Rules

Lesson Objective:

At the end of the lesson, the student should:

1. Be able to compile several exceptions to the general rules under *RONR (12ᵗʰ ed.)*.

2. Understand the rationale behind the exception.

Lesson Setup:

1. The student should bring a copy of *RONR (12ᵗʰ ed.)*

2. The students are required to provide exceptions that apply to the more general rule and determine the usefulness of the exception. In addition, they cite the reference in *RONR (12ᵗʰ ed.)*.

3. The workshop leader decides whether the questions are answered one question at a time or as a total assignment. Optionally the workshop leader may assign groups of questions to groups of students. In either case the students report back in a plenary session and discuss the answers.

4. As a final exercise, the students should identify up to five other exceptions that they are aware of and cite the reference to them in *RONR (12ᵗʰ ed.)*.

5. Only the workshop leader has the answer sheet but provides copies to all students at the end of the lesson.

Lesson Reference Material:

1. *RONR (12ᵗʰ ed.)*

2. Exceptions to the Rules (provided)

3. Answers to Exceptions to the Rules (provided).

Exceptions to the Rules:

I.   List at least one exception to the following general rules. Cite the exception in *RONR (12th ed.)*. Identify how the exception might be useful.

1. A member can make only one motion at a time.

2. Adoption of a main motion requires only a majority vote.

3. A main motion must be seconded before it is stated by the chair.

4. A motion to *Reconsider* may be made only by one who voted with the prevailing side.

5. After a motion is stated by the chair, the mover cannot withdraw or modify it as it now is the property of the assembly.

6. A motion to *Limit or Extend Limits of Debate* may be applied to any debatable motion.

7. An amendment of the third degree is not permitted.

8. A motion to *Recess* is a privileged motion.

9. An appeal may be made to any ruling by the presiding officer.

10. If *Object to Consideration of a Question* is sustained, the motion is dismissed.

11. The first item on the agenda should be the reading of the minutes.

12. A member's vote can be changed up until the time the chair announces the result.

13. A member may have only one vote.

14. An adopted or rejected motion cannot be considered again during the same session.

15. A report of committee contains only that which was agreed to by a majority vote at a properly called meeting, a quorum being present.

16. Reports are received by the membership for information.

17. Delegates to convention are free to vote as they see fit.

18. A committee can appoint a sub-committee.

19. A substitute is a primary amendment

20. If a quorum is not present, no business may be transacted.

21. Not more than two motions can be pending at the same time, as amendments.

22. The chair, as a member of the assembly has the same rights to debate as any other member.

23. All illegal votes are taken into account in determining the number of votes cast for the purpose of determining a majority.

24. The right to vote is limited to the members who are actually present at a legal meeting.

25. Illegal votes are not included in a tellers' report.

26. A committee acts for the society only on specific instructions.

27. Motions that require a two-thirds vote should not be decided by a voice vote (*viva voce*).

28. To *Rescind* requires a two-thirds vote for adoption.

29. A motion to *Reconsider* may be applied to the motion *Object to Consideration of a Question.*

30. The first to rise and address the chair must have first right to speak.

II.   Each student now identifies five additional exceptions to the rules, citing a reference in *RONR (12ᵗʰ ed.)* and explains the rationale behind the exception.

Answers to Exceptions to the Rules:

1. A member can make only one motion at a time.

   RONR (12th ed.), p. 2625:42. When the purpose of a motion to *Suspend the Rules* is to permit the making of another motion, and the adoption of the first motion would obviously be followed by adoption of the second, the two motions can be combined, ...The foregoing is an exception to the general rule that no member can make two motions at the same time except with the consent of the assembly - unanimous consent being required if the two motions are unrelated. ***RONR (12th ed.), 10:25.*** A series of resolutions offered at once, ***RONR (12th ed.), 19:1.*** A question of privilege raised as a main motion.

2. Adoption of a main motion requires only a majority vote.

   RONR (12th ed.), 35:2(7). To *Rescind* and to *Amend Something Previously Adopted* require a two-thirds vote if previous notice has not been given.

3. A main motion must be seconded before it is stated by the chair.

   RONR (12th ed.), 51:11. Motions coming out of committee need not be seconded, assumed motions (**51:12,51:30** for example) need not be seconded, nominations (**46:6**) and the motion to adopt the recommendations in a committee report (**51:11**). The motion in the latter case may be assumed.

4. A motion to *Reconsider* may be made only by one who voted with the prevailing side.

   RONR (12th ed.), 37:35(2). In committee, anyone who did not vote with the losing side, even one who abstained or was absent at the time the vote was taken, may move to reconsider.

5. After a motion is stated by the chair, the mover cannot withdraw or modify it as it now is the property of the assembly.

   RONR (12th ed.), 33:13-15. A member may withdraw a motion if permission is given by unanimous (general) consent. ***RONR (12th ed.), p. 76:17(11c).*** It is considered a request.

6. A motion to *Limit or Extend Limits of Debate* may be applied to any debatable motion.

   RONR (12th ed.), 49:22(3)(n3). *Limit or Extend Limits of Debate* is generally not in order in small boards and committees.

7. An amendment of the third degree is not permitted.

   RONR (12th ed.), 12:92. See **Filling Blanks.**

8. A motion to *Recess* is a privileged motion.

   RONR (12th ed.), 20:3. Except when moved when no business is pending. As such it becomes a main motion, debatable, and subject to the same rules as other main motions.

9. An appeal may be made to any ruling by the presiding officer.

   RONR (12th ed.), 24:6-7. Except that of *Parliamentary Inquiry* wherein the chair gives an opinion, not a ruling, nor on announcements of the result of a vote. *Division of the Assembly* can be used in this case if there is doubt of the vote.

10. If *Object to Consideration of a Question* is sustained, the motion is dismissed.

    RONR (12th ed.), 36:6. A sustained *Objection to the Consideration of a Question* may be reconsidered.

11. The first item on the agenda should be the reading of the minutes.

    RONR (12th ed.), 3:16(1), 41:9. Opening exercises may precede the reading of the minutes. If the minutes have been distributed prior to the meeting the oral reading is sometimes dispensed with or there may have been a motion to dispense with the reading of the minutes.

12. A member's vote can be changed up until the time the chair announces the result.

    RONR (12th ed.), 45:18-23. Voting by *ballot* ... is used when secrecy of the members' votes is desired.....When a vote is to be taken, or has been taken, by ballot, whether or not the bylaws require that form of voting, no motion is in order that would force the disclosure of a member's vote or views on the matter. Secrecy of the ballot is key. If the vote is by ballot, there is no way to identify the ballot.

    (Note: ***AIPSC,*** p. **157.** When voting is by ballot, a member may not change the ballot after it has been placed in the ballot box.)

13. A member may have only one vote.

    RONR (12th ed.), 45:62-69. Preferential ballot gives the member multiple choices.

    RONR (12th ed.), 45:70-71. Proxy holders may have many votes, some members such as Honorary, Associate, may have no vote. In some corporations, shareholders vote in proportion to the shares they own.

    RONR (12th ed.), 46:43. Cumulative voting gives a member the opportunity to cast more than one vote for one or more candidates.

14. An adopted or rejected motion cannot be considered again during the same session.

RONR (12ᵗʰ ed.), **35:1, 37:1**. Parliamentary motions that bring a question again before the assembly, such as to *Rescind, Reconsider,* and *Amend Something Previously Adopted* may be used to bring back a motion that has been previously voted on.

15. A report of committee contains only that which was agreed to by a majority vote at a properly called meeting, a quorum being present.

RONR (12ᵗʰ ed.), **51:2**. When a committee cannot meet because of distance or other circumstances a report can be made on the basis of separate consultations with every member and the official report can then be made on what was agreed to by every one of its members. If the committee members are expected to do their work by correspondence, the report can contain only what is agreed to by a majority of its members.

16. Reports are received by the membership for information.

RONR (12ᵗʰ ed.), **51:10**. Except when they contain recommendations that are acted upon or, on occasion, when there is a motion to adopt (endorse) an entire report.

17. Delegates to convention are free to vote as they see fit.

RONR (12ᵗʰ ed.), **58:18**. Except when they are given instructions from the constituent unit. This is not considered good practice.

18. A committee can appoint a sub-committee.

RONR (12ᵗʰ ed.), **5**.:15 Except in committee of the whole.

19. A substitute is a primary amendment

RONR (12ᵗʰ ed.), **57:4**. A substitute may be a main motion, as in amending bylaws. *RONR (12ᵗʰ ed.),* **12:69 footnote 6**. Also a substitute may be a secondary amendment.

20. If a quorum is not present, no business may be transacted.

RONR (12ᵗʰ ed.), **40:6-7**. Except the motions to *Adjourn, Fix a Time to Which to Adjourn,* or to *Recess;* or to take measures necessary to obtain a quorum. Subsidiary and incidental motions, questions of privilege, motions to *Raise a Question of Privilege* or *Call for Orders of the Day,* and other motions may also be considered if they are related to these motions or to the conduct of the meeting while it remains without a quorum.

21. Not more than two motions can be pending at the same time, as amendments.

    RONR (12th ed.), 12:79. Amendments may be offered to both the original version of a proposed motion and to the proposed substitute.

    RONR (12th ed.), 12:92-113. When filling blanks, each of several alternatives is equivalent to a motion to amend and it is possible to apply higher ranking subsidiary and privileged motions to the main motion, and then have first and second degree amendments to any amendable motion; secondary amendments may be pending on the original and the substitute in the case of amending by substitution.

22. The chair, as a member of the assembly has the same rights to debate as any other member.

    RONR (12th ed.), 43:29. Except that impartiality in presiding require the chair to preclude the exercise of some of the chair's rights as a member.

23. All illegal votes are taken into account in determining the number of votes cast for the purpose of determining a majority.

    RONR (12th ed.), 45:32. Yes. All ballots that indicate a preference - provided that they have been cast by persons entitled to vote - are taken into account in determining the number of votes cast for the purposes of computing the majority.

    (Note that ***AIPSC, pp. 167-168,*** does not provide that illegal ballots are taken into account when determining the number of votes cast for the purposes of computing the majority. Only legal ballots are counted.)

24. The right to vote is limited to the members who are actually present at a legal meeting.

    RONR (12th ed.), 45:56. Except if bylaws stipulate otherwise, as in cases where the vote is by mail or in proxy voting.

25. Illegal votes are not included in a tellers' report.

    RONR (12th ed.), 45:32. The tellers' report indicates the number of illegal votes.

    (Note: ***AIPSC, p. 167,*** illegal votes are not included in a teller's report.)

26. A committee acts for the society only on specific instructions.

    RONR (12th ed.), 50:5. Except when appointed "with power."

27. Motions that require a two-thirds vote should not be decided by a voice vote (*viva voce*).

RONR (12ᵗʰ ed.), **4:58-60**. If there is unanimous consent (no one objects), such motions as close nominations, change the order of business, or amend a standing rule without notice may be decided without putting the motion to a formal vote.

28. To *Rescind* requires a two-thirds vote for adoption.

   RONR (12ᵗʰ ed.), **35:2(7)**. Rescind may be adopted by a majority with previous notice or by the vote of a majority of the entire membership.

29. A motion to *Reconsider* may be applied to the motion *Object to Consideration of a Question.*

   RONR (12ᵗʰ ed.), **26:6**. The motion to *Reconsider* may not be applied to *Object to Consideration* if it has been voted to consider the question. (*Reconsider* may be applied only to a negative vote – that is, to a vote <u>sustaining</u> the objection.)

30. The first to rise and address the chair must have first right to speak.

   RONR (12ᵗʰ ed.), **4:27.** The maker of the motion has first rights to debate if he claims it before anyone else has been recognized, even if someone else has risen and addressed the chair first.

Each student now identifies five additional exceptions to the rules, citing a reference in *RONR (12ᵗʰ ed.)* and explains the rationale behind the exception.

This page intentionally left blank.